AF413653

Rearview Reflections

of Arlington, Texas

Short Stories Looking Back on Growing Up in
Arlington, Texas in the '50s & '60s

Danny Armstrong

Rearview Reflections
of Arlington, Texas

Short Stories Looking Back on Growing Up in
Arlington, Texas in the '50s & '60s

ISBN (paperback) 979-8-8722-6972-4
ISBN (hardcover) 979-8-8692-4593-9

Cover design and book layout by DTPerfect Book Design

Introduction

After WWII, Arlington, Texas was a small, north Texas town, located midway between Dallas and Ft. Worth. My family moved there in 1948 and the population was about 7,000. At that time Arlington had many small businesses, a college, two elementary schools, one high school, a handful of restaurants and many churches. It became fairly rural a short distance out of town. The town grew rapidly with the expansion of large aircraft companies as well as many new big companies like American Can Company and General Motors. As predicted, in the late '50s and '60s the population exploded. This booklet is a compilation of short stories relating to growing up in Arlington during the '50s & '60s through my eyes.

I hope you enjoy the stories and if you wish to communicate please do so via email: dannozz63@yahoo.com

Best Wishes,
Danny

Baby Boomer Coming of Age
Stories in Arlington, Texas

I was in the Arlington HS Class of 1963 and now live in Santa Fe, NM with my AHS sweetheart, Becky.

This booklet is my recollection of stories while growing up in Arlington during the '50s and '60s. Enjoy the trip back in time.

Danny

Table of Contents

STORIES BY DANNY ARMSTRONG

We Were So Fortunate!

To grow up in the '50s and '60s in Arlington, Texas. Talk about good luck! All of us kids of the 1950s and 1960s who grew up in Arlington, Texas, were the most fortunate of all kids before and after, hands down! The war was over. Aircraft and auto manufacturing companies were moving into the North Texas economic area. We had cheap land, plentiful labor, and low taxes. The new opportunities were abundant and the big corporations doubled down. All the new families, from many areas of the country were thrown together, as the companies moved in their crucial management teams, and became stronger for it. As a community, we were thrown and bonded together, growing to meet the challenges of the future. We were not faced with climate change issues nor with racial prejudice. Like other kids, my concern was "What's for supper" and "When can I drive". The balance of politics was almost insignificant! I think those concerns are still relevant!! I still really want to know what's for dinner! Elvis was a big deal and Sinatra was getting older. Gunsmoke and Bonanza were prime time as was a rather new thing, televised sports! Bucket seats were becoming popular as well as high-performance engines and four-speed floor shift transmissions.

What a period in time! After WWII, South Side and North Side (later renamed Kooken) were the only elementary schools in town. Maxie Speer and West Side were yet to come. Coach Mayfield Workman, in 1947 had just been hired as an assistant coach to help bring Arlington High into State recognition. Coach Workman had a task, but he had great support from the community, the entire Goodwin and Hollingsworth families, and all of the AHS Colt brotherhood. He was successful!

GM came to town in 1952, thanks to our great mayor, Tommy Vandergriff, and the town boomed. Arlington State College still played ball in the old, stone-encircled stadium, coached by Chena Gilstrap. Arlington was indeed in a transition. From a little rural town of 4,500 folks after the war, we were growing at an astounding rate. By 1957 we were about 10,000 folks. The nearby aircraft companies of Chance Vought, Bell, and General Dynamics along with General Motors had evolved Arlington into a dynamic metropolis. What once was a quiet little suburb was now a thriving economic center. As time evolved, Tommy V., sadly, no longer called the AHS football games at the ASC, stone-walled stadium, and the stadium came down.

Back to the center of my point: what a great place to grow up! We could ride our bikes all over town. "Just be home for supper" was our mother's command. In the summer we could ride bikes over to South Side School for a fun activity. They had a fire escape from the second floor that was a huge, curved, "playground" slide, like a half-pipe! We could climb up and slide down. It was a sad day when they tore it down! We could ride west toward the future Lake Arlington and watch the earth movers working. Some of the equipment would be abandoned as they could not get it out in time when the flood water came rushing in, pre-maturity, to fill the big hole in 1957. We could ride south, beyond the triangle of pines at Park Row, all the way past South Davis School to Johnson Station. And, on occasion, we would go north, past Al's Drive-In on North Collins, beyond where they were beginning to build the new DFW Turnpike. Always home by supper! But, on one occasion we were running late. Luckily we hailed down a pickup truck. The truck, a beautiful white and red 1957 Chevy Cameo, was driven by Ted Arnold, a future driver for Vance Hunt, AA Fuel Dragster Champion. Go figure! Nice guy and we were saved!

The thing that is most amazing to me about that time, was the literal spider web of personal connections we had in a small town. If the kid wasn't in my church, or kindergarten, or grade school, or little league team, or Cub Scouts, or Mrs. Carlson's swim class, or in the neighborhood, or if his parents didn't know my parents, it was an absolute miracle! That kid must be new! Anyway, I am so thankful to have been a part of growing Arlington, at that time and for those friends. So many "Friends for Life", literally! What a blessing. Thanks, friends!

Danny Armstrong
ABC Class of 1950
West Side School
Ousley Jr. High
AHS Class of 1963

2

ABC Kindergarten Class 1950

It was 1950 in Arlington, Texas. I was in Lila Houston's ABC Kindergarten class on South West Street just south of West Main Street. It was an old wooden house facing East in exactly the south parking lot area of Wally Hardin's, The Man's Shop, formerly Eddie Williams Men's Store, on the corner of West and Main. Lila was Reford Houston's wife and Jimmy and Brice Houston's aunt. Whitey was a few years older and was Lila and Reford's son. I knew this great family through The First Presbyterian Church initially on West Abram then in a new location on South Collins by 1956.

The original house must have been built in the 1930s and may have been the family home place. It had a small front yard, a large front porch, a rather big open area for the desks, and a big backyard full of big oak trees. I don't remember much grass in the backyard as the herds of kids must have beaten it down. There was limited play equipment and there was a sandbox. As I recall it was half days, maybe four days a week. We'd have character dress-up days, music days, painting days, and of course reading and printing curriculums. Mrs. Houston and her helpers did a great job helping to prepare us for first grade.

One of my favorite classmates was Stewart DeVore. Stewart's dad used to take us to ABC some mornings. We lived near each other in the College Hills subdivision. Mr. DeVore drove a new 1951 (purchased in 1950) Chrysler New Yorker equipped with Chrysler's new 331 cubic inch Hemi V8! Stewart and I would coerce Mr. DeVore to "floor it" on occasion, and he would oblige. It made for fun trips to kindergarten!

One special day we got to go to the fire station. The Chief, Mr. Dunlop, showed us the fire trucks and all around, including the firemen's quarters, the equipment room, and the kitchen. It was a great field trip and we could walk to the station from our school. A fun time was had by all.

Another day we went to the library not far down the street on West Main, not far from the mineral water well, right by the Rockefeller hamburger restaurant. We had to be quiet when we went inside. The librarian ladies were nice. We got to tour the entire building and there were books everywhere. There were more books than any of us had ever seen!

It was a great year for us young Arlingtonites. I got to make new friends that would be infinitely important as we all moved from the kiddie pool into slightly deeper water.

Thanks, Mrs. Houston,
Danny
1950

3

A Typical Saturday in 1955

All Saturdays were fun in Arlington, Texas in 1955. But about once a month we'd have a special Saturday. After a breakfast of hotcakes and bacon with orange juice, Billy (Dad), Johnny, and I would leave home at about 9:00 AM and go to downtown Arlington. At that time, our sister Jan stayed with Mom as she was a little young for our escapades. We had places to go and people to see! Back then, everywhere we wanted to go was within about a two-block radius of South Center and Abram. We'd go to the bank first on that same corner. Dad knew many of the tellers so we would say hi and wave to all three of them. Next, on to the Electric Company with the big Ready Kilowatt mascot sign out front. Then to the Lone Star Gas Company, then to Southwestern Bell, the phone company. Ok, the chores were done and the bills were paid, now we could get to the fun things! There was White's Auto, a wonderful conglomeration of mechanical and electrical devices from hammers to power lawnmowers and chainsaws, as well as a huge assortment of tools. An absolute haven!! There was Caton's Five & Dime on the east side of the center and next door was Eddie Williams Men's Store. We'd say hello to Mr. Williams as he was a very nice man. North of Caton's was

Mr. Fred Bondurant's small insurance office. Mr. Bondurant and Dad were old friends having met at Texas A&M in the '40s. There was Terry Brothers Drug, which included a soda fountain with awesome strawberry milkshakes, at the intersection of Main & Center. The round fountain/mineral water well was in the middle of that intersection as well. Rockefeller's Hamburgers was just to the west of the library on Main. And Mr. Brice's barber shop just south of The Francine Shop on the west side of the Center, for haircuts. Walking those downtown sidewalks we'd usually run into Marshall Morton. Marshall was a young man, probably 15 years my senior. He was always patrolling the streets of downtown Arlington, keeping the peace. He always wore a superb cowboy outfit complete with two pistols, a big ten-gallon hat, and fancy boots with spurs. He was Arlington's honorary sheriff! He would greet us, cordially ask us about our business in his town today, show off his quick draw, comment on the day, and bid us goodbye, as well as a Marshall's warning: "Don't cause any trouble in my town today, boys", warning. With that comment, we all answered "Yes sir, we won't cause any trouble". That was the right answer as Marshall tipped his hat and we passed. Many times we'd go to Binion's Lumber Yard on West Street. It was always our last stop as we bought supplies for some new project. Looking back, it was all truly a unique and memorable experience growing up in a small town.

We'd be home for lunch and do our house and yard chores in the afternoon. We'd likely have 30 minutes of catch, be it baseball or football, and then, sometime in the afternoon, I'd go for a spin on the Schwinn around Varsity Circle to check on friends. For supper, we might go to LaTapatia, a Mexican food restaurant on the corner of West and Division. It was run by two sisters and was the best Mexican food in our area. Of course, Johnny and I would "wolf" through our dinners and be ready to go before Mom was halfway through. After Mom was finished with her meal she would always ask for coffee. Finally, after a long time, Mom was ready. We were anxious to get home and watch our favorite westerns on TV. But first, The Dinah Shore Chevy Show, for Mom and Jan. When Dinah was over we could get down to Wagon Train, then the 20 Mule Team Borax Show with Ronald Reagan, then Bonanza with Adam and Hoss and Little Joe! During the shows, we'd shine shoes for church the next day. When TV ended we get showered and hit the hay. Another great Saturday in Arlington!

Great Memories,
Danny

4

Career Night Open House

At Arlington State College, Circa 1952

We moved to Arlington in 1948 when my dad, Billy, accepted a position at ASC, as an Industrial Arts teacher. He taught wood shop, metal shop, and mechanical drawing. We were moving from Laurel, Mississippi and I had a new baby brother, Johnny. I'll never forget the first time we saw the campus as a family. It must have been in June or July as the orange/yellow cannas were in bloom all around the campus, as well as the mimosa trees with pink blossoms. We had a black 1939 Buick at that time and my dad had replaced the five radio station selector buttons, that had spelled Buick, with the letters of my name. Funny, the little things we remember.

Back then ASC was a relatively small campus, all in an area of about six square blocks with South Cooper on the west and South Oak Street on the east. There were athletic dorms and the stone-walled football stadium just west of Cooper. There were also some animal husbandry facilities further west of South Davis, where the new Maverick stadium was built a few decades later. In 1948 the population of Arlington was about 7,000.

In the summer, during that timeframe, it was customary for ASC to host a Career Night Open House. Each of the schools of the college would create displays and demonstrations in order to attract kids from all nearby areas to come to see what ASC had to offer. The prospective students could learn a little bit about the programs that were available and even meet and visit with their potential teachers. Makes sense in a lot of ways. Now, I was just a youngster when Dad was at the college and he was participating in these activities. I'm certain the schools of history and English had their particular appeal to many of the near-adult guests, however, to me, as a kid, the fun exhibits were in the engineering area as well as the Industrial Arts areas. They were fun! It was kind of a carnival atmosphere!

That particular evening it was just me and Mom, as Johnny was with a sitter. First, we went to the History Department, and there we found nice graphics about the wars our country had fought. It must have been pretty good as I thought Mom would never leave. Next was English. At seven, I wondered who the heck was William Shakespeare. Later, I got to know them and concluded he was my kind of guy! We saw Mr. Shupe and Mr. Smith along the way. Then we made it to the Engineering school display. They had exhibits of the atomic bomb and rocket propulsion. Great for me as I was really into those things at age seven! Finally, we are through with the prelims and on to the main events: Metallurgy, wood shop, metal shop, and baking sciences (my favorite), after all, I had been here before!

First, we went to Metallurgy Sciences. Our friend Mr. Stiles, was the main teacher. It was fun. These guys melted different recipes of metal together to get a better combination of what they had before. Then they poured the liquid metal into a form to get the desired part. It was cool to watch. For the presentation that evening they were melting an aluminum mixture and casting the metal into forms yielding small medallions they gave away as souvenirs. Like small coins. I still have one! Next, we made our way to the "Wood Tech", or Wood Shop! There were three guys working on wood lathes making miniature whiskey barrels made into toothpick holders. They were incredible little souvenirs that were made in about four minutes. The smell of the wood being cut and burnished was somewhat intoxicating, although I didn't understand that sensation as a seven-year-old! Next, we went to the Metal Technologies Studies. In that class, they learned how to fabricate metal parts and assemblies. That year the students were making miniature ball-peen hammers for souvenirs. The hammers were made of two parts, the head and the handle. By heating the head and cooling the handle they could press the two parts together. Very interesting, even for young kids. I still have one.

Then, last stop, saving the best for last, Baking Technologies! My favorite. Our friend, Mr. Scottino (Scotty) ran this department and was the best "cooker" I'd ever known. I told him so! Likely not too impressive to receive a seven-year-old, however, I think he appreciated it. Anything he made was the best ever! That evening he was making doughnuts. I had one then convinced Mom I needed another. Unforgettable! Thanks, Scotty!

Those open house events were very memorable and fun, as well as informative to prospective students.

Thanks to all,
Danny

5

Trouble with the Principal! (Almost)

I was in the 5th grade at West Side School in Arlington, Texas, circa 1956.

This is a short one, I promise. It was a great year as I had Mrs. Stanford. She was a great teacher and was a friend of the family! However, she cut me no slack. She had two daughters, Beverly, one year older than me, and Carol, three years younger, the same age as Johnny, my brother. Mr. Bebense was the Principal. Super guy! I had a few interactions with him. Always fair! Perhaps not what I wanted at the time, but fair! We had an incredible custodian, Mr. Heinze, and that is what we called him. He lived at the corner of Benge and South Davis, across from Saint Maria Goretti Catholic Church and School. (I loved that name: I could say it over and over, and the girls that went there, ooh-la-la!) At any rate, Mr. Heinze took great pride in the manner in which he kept the facility, especially in the way he buffed and waxed the floors into an absolute epitome of cleanliness and shine, second to none, even to those of a hospital. The hallways of West Side were in a 90-degree "V" shape about 130' each way.

Anyway, my friend Larry Mazo and I, somehow came up with the same brilliant idea at the same time. Actually, it was magical!! We had to ride our bikes on that incredibly smooth, perfect surface. Just to glide on such a surface would be phenomenal. Never before or after could we experience such a feeling. We had to do it!

We picked a day, Friday at 3:45. Everyone was gone. It was time and we were ready! What a ride! It was heaven. Talk about a smooth ride! What an experience! We powered down one hallway, then the next, and repeated the process, probably six times then we skedaddled out of the building! We were very careful not to scratch the floors or the walls. We did no damage as we knew there would be severe consequences if we did. No witnesses! We were home free, we thought.

Come Monday, we were on thin ice. Mr. Heinze had noticed what appeared to be bicycle tire tracks on his floors. It was like Dragnet. Mr. Heinze was angry, he felt violated! An intercom announcement came across the speakers later that day indicating that riding bikes inside the building was prohibited. It certainly was assuring to receive that direction as previously it had been unclear, certainly to Larry and me. We never admitted the gruesome act, nor did we lie, nor did we damage anything. I felt bad, but not that bad, what a ride!! A once in a life time experience!

Thanks, Larry,
Danny

6

Little League Baseball

*An absolute Godsend for us guys growing up
in Arlington in the '50s and '60s!*

Not sure what the Arlington girls had to occupy their time in the summer but, the guys had Little League Baseball, and what an absolute blessing it was! For us to be able to learn from our coaches, to actually get better at our given positions, and then to compete against our friends on opposing teams, what could be more fun? About April each year, our thoughts turned to baseball. It started when we were about nine or ten years old through twelve. Perhaps Santa had brought us a new Ted Williams glove or a Lou Gehrig bat for Christmas and we were anxious to try it out. Or maybe, Uncle Bob promised us a new glove when the practice started. No matter what, we were anxious for each new season to begin.

We were fortunate to have an excellent, almost new Little League facility named Senter Park on South Mary, just across from the cemetery. There were two beautiful diamonds complete with grass infields and outfields, lights, wooden fences, sunken dugouts, scoreboards, bleachers, restrooms, and a concession stand! It was heaven! The facility was owned by the city but leased, operated, and maintained by the local Optimist Club. Little League teams began playing ball at the new facility in the summer of 1953. Arlington had four divisions, defined geographically, with about eight teams per division. Some of the team names were: Lumberjacks, Tigers, Giants, Little Deacons, Closers, Tornadoes, Ready Kilowatts, and the Rotary Wheels. There were many others but their names escape me. The games were competitive and fun. Afterward, many families would congregate at the Chuck Wagon Drive-in on East Division for burgers and milkshakes.

Maybe our off-season practice would pay off in the hitting department or catching or running. Maybe this year we'd be able to hit that darned fastball from Teddy Moore or be able to get a hit by that rascal Charlie Jobe at short. Or even, maybe score a run on the menace of the home plate, Rusty Workman! At any rate, we had plenty of very worthy opponents in every game. There were many great players on opposing teams other than those mentioned above such as Dennis Carlson, Jack Merbler, Lee Roy Mitchell, Charles McAlpine, Joe Skelton, Mike Hedlund, (a future Pro), Jay Wood, Robert McDonald, Royce Bush, Gerald Baker, Ronnie McCain, Bobby Godfrey and many, many more. On the flip side, we were fairly worthy opponents for most teams. They had to get by Stewart's fastball as well as slip one by Nicky Joy at short or Bob Rose at second. Lee Hart at second was awesome as well. Tony Bastone played catcher and was hard to steal on. Of course, Pat Mahan at third was a handful. And Danny Armstrong (yours truly) at pitcher was a little unpredictable. Was the fastball going to hit you or skid by for a strike? Your guess! I remember my worst game. I walked the bases loaded, then walked two more. It was a bad night and a seat on the bench was waiting for me!! We had a great team in 1955 and we all had tons of fun! Other team members included Randy Rogers, Larry Mazo,

Ronny Grimes, Dennis Niles, Jerald Demery, and Roland Ross. We were fortunate, as were all teams, to have several up-and-coming ball players. Our newcomers were Andy Hibbitts, Don Tucker, Johnny MacDonald, Johnny Higgins, Wade Skiles, and Don Kitchen. Kids played Little League until they were twelve, then they went on to Junior League then Senior League. As we aged and continued playing it was still fun but not like Little League!

Great memories forever!! Thanks, guys, Coaches, and Optimist Club!
Danny

The Renowned "Witch June"

Spook House of 1957, Arlington, Texas

It was Halloween in 1957. We still lived on University Drive in the College Hills neighborhood. Since the two-bedroom house was a little small for our three-kid family, Dad designed an addition comprised of a large (at least it seemed large at the time) master suite that had been dried in, but not finished on the inside. The interior walls were framed but without sheet-rock and the sub-floor was in place. It was safe to play in as we had a ping pong table there, a train layout, and other toys. My Mom, June, thought it would be fun to turn it into a spook house for the neighborhood kids for Halloween. We all agreed! So a couple of weeks early she began planning it out. We had tons of kids in the six-to-ten-year-old range, so that was the "targeted" visitor.

This was the plan. Mom would be "Witch June", dressed in a black robe, black pointed hat, and facial and hand makeup. The entire lair portion of the spook house would be dark except for a few candles and small flashlights. There would be dry ice fog filling the area, as well as spooky sounds from a tape recorder. My buddy Larry and I would be the gatekeepers and would take the kids, one or two at a time, back into the witch's lair, if the kids elected to do so. The ones that didn't, we would just give them candy. Dad would provide the "scare" effect on the way to the lair, all dressed in black, reaching through the wood-framed walls, laughing, and making other scary noises. Once to the lair, which was a separate area (the unfinished master bath), the kid would be introduced to "Witch June". She would reach out her ugly hand with ultra-long, fake nails and ask them to close their eyes. Witch June would have peeled grapes for eyeballs, slimy spaghetti for worms, and peeled apples depicting monkey heads. She would ask them to feel each of the items in the bowls and to guess what each bowl contained. At the end of the session Witch June would give them a special treat. Then, Larry and I would lead them out the back door. The plan sounded good.

Halloween came and it was a cool, beautiful, full-moon evening. We were ready! Kids started coming. The plan worked perfectly! I'm certain that some of the kids from the neighborhood still remember "Witch June" from that evening!

After the traffic died down, Larry and I made a few rounds of the neighborhood and contemplated visiting the chapel and baby graveyard at the Berachah Home for Erring and Outcast Girls, HOWEVER, we decided against that and made our way home.

Thanks for a very memorable Halloween!!
Danny

8

Summer Vacation Trip with Beryl, 1957

It was the summer of 1957. At that time my grandmother Beryl lived in Houston and worked for Hughes Tool Company. She was a "character" to say the least. She loved to tell slightly dirty jokes and actually survived pancreatic cancer. She loved bowling, cards, and most other games. She was tough but sweet. She had raised her only child, Billy, single-handedly, without any fatherly assistance from her ex-husband. Then, when Billy went to the Army in 1942, from Texas A&M, she joined the WACS. After the war, she had a good job as a comptometer operator for Hughes, there in Houston. She loved fast and pretty cars. In the '50s she would show up at our house, by surprise, every couple of years with a new Mercury, her car of choice that decade. They came in hardtop models with pretty color combinations and with more powerful engines than Ford. Beryl had a '52, '54, '56 and '57 that decade.

The "Big M" as we called the '57, had a lavish interior and even sported a tachometer. It was the coolest as it was a tri-tone, red/black/white Turnpike Cruiser model with a 368 c.i. engine, 4-barrel carb, and dual exhausts. It had a push-button gear selector, quad headlights, a powered breezeway rear windshield, and fancy hubcaps. There was a large, gold "M" in the center of the grill. For a large car, it seemed pretty fast, at least to me, and Beryl would turn those horses loose on the highway! She could not stand for anyone to be ahead of her on the open road!

Ok, so it was the summer of '57 and she had the new Turnpike Cruiser so Beryl decided that she would take each of her three grandchildren on a one-week summer vacation trip when they were 11 or 12. I was 12 and was first the first kid to go. We were going to The Grand Canyon! I had a tiny suitcase and my Chicago Roller Skates in their own pink and black case, just in case we found a roller rink. I had saved up $60.00 and was ready to go.

The next day we headed out early. We got to Amarillo early afternoon then connected with Route 66 and headed west. Our journey would take us to The Petrified Forest, west of Gallup, then to Flagstaff, then north to the Grand Canyon, then back to Arlington. We were on our way. Outside of Amarillo, heading west on Route 66 toward Gallup, we passed a trucker rolling along about 80. I asked Beryl if she knew how fast the "Big M" would go. She said "I don't know yet but let's find out! Hang on!" She rolled that "Big M" right up to the peg. I thought I was in heaven! Quickly she slowed her down to about 85 and we cruised on to Gallup and stopped for the day. On a couple of occasions, when the highway was clear, Beryl would let me scoot over toward her and push on the gas with my left foot. I could feel those horses yearning to run free! Awesome!

Back then, there were always little roadside motels so as we pulled into Gallup we spotted one that looked nice and clean with a cafe beside it. We got checked in to the "Gallup On Inn" and walked next door to "Roy's Cowboy Diner". While we were checking out the menu, an ad on the table caught my attention. "Sally's Skate Haven" was just a few blocks away and Beryl was happy for us to go there after supper,, after all, I had my Chicago skates cleaned up, oiled, and ready to go! Sally's was a cool little rink and I got to have a lot of fun. I won a couple of races and met a girl named Jennifer. She and I got to have a few "couples" skates. It was a very serendipitous (and you didn't think I knew that word) evening. If timing worked out, Beryl said we might get to stop there again on the way back home.

The next morning off to Flagstaff, then north to the Grand Canyon. We got there at the end of the day and checked into the "Bright Angel Lodge". It was a really nice place built in 1935 and overlooking the south rim of the Grand Canyon. The next morning, after breakfast, we went on a burro ride down into the canyon. It was a long ride and took us almost the entire day. It became a little boring for me but I sure didn't want to walk back up to the top! It was a very interesting ride as the scenery was breathtaking. We got back to the lodge, had nice showers, and went to supper. We both slept very well that night.

The next day we were off to see the Petrified Forest, then back to Gallup. We had changed our schedule in order to hit Sally's again. Another fun evening at Sally's and Jennifer managed to be there as well. Great night and a safe journey home.

Those were the highlights of a very fun week with my very fun grandmother Beryl and the "Big M", as well as beautiful sunsets and amazing geological formations! I thought to myself "Maybe I'll be back"!

R.I.P. Beryl.
Love you,
Danny

9

The Boating Experience, 1958

Lake Arlington was full and officially open for outdoor fun. Johnny and I were pressuring Dad for a boat. What fun we could have skiing and doing all sorts of other fun things in the water! And hey, the lake was nearby so it wouldn't be too much trouble to get there. Of course, we would help with the "getting ready" preparations as well as the "cleaning up" chores after the given outing. Dad was in, now only to convince Mom. We concentrated on the "together as a family" aspects of the endeavor and of course, we'd always wear life jackets. Success!

It just so happened that there was a boat dealer on East Division, a little east of Candlelite Inn on the same side of Division. The name of the place was appropriately Arlington Marine Sales & Service. Mr. Robert Jones was the owner. He was a very nice man and sold all sorts of boat parts and accessories, as well as new outboard motors and some used boats. We looked around a little but the newer boats seemed out of our reach, budget-wise, and the older ones were really older and needed way too much work. Just as we were about to leave, Mr. Jones said there was one more we should look at. He was in the process of rebuilding her, but his progress had halted due to his increased workload. He had her in a separate shed out back. He opened the door and there she was. A 16-foot-long, wooden princess! She needed a lot of work but it was wood and fiberglass work we could do in our garage. She had a 35-horsepower Johnson, with a pull start. The best part: it was well within the budget! Done deal! Dad named her "June Bug". (June's mom, Pallie, used to call her that as a kid).

We got her home and began work. We turned the boat over and rested it on supports, in our one-car garage to facilitate the work. The entire hull had to be stripped of paint, any bad wood replaced, then totally fiberglassed, and finally, painted. It took us many evenings and weekends to complete the project. The work turned out fine and we were proud of our accomplishment.

We all were anxious for the next warm Saturday to go test her out. The big day came. We loaded up with the supplies and tools we thought we might need. We stopped for gas and precisely measured the oil to go in her fuel tank. (Back then you had to manually add the oil to the gas as the tank was filled). We stopped at the State Boat Inspection office to get the appropriate license, then we backed her down the boat ramp into the water. We off-loaded her from the trailer and tied her off at the pier. We knew the engine would run as we tested it at home with the propeller in a garbage can filled with water. At the time we were the only ones at the ramp/dock, which later turned out to be a good thing!

Dad and Johnny were with the boat and I was parking the car/trailer in the designated lot on Arkansas Lane. As I was walking toward the dock, a crazy thing happened that caused me to begin running. Dad was in the boat trying to get the motor started. The nose of the boat happened to be pointed toward the dock where Johnny was standing. All of a sudden the little motor had started. The problem was that none of us realized the motor would start in gear as well as in neutral. It was in the forward gear. The motor roared as the throttle was partially open. "June Bug" jumped the dock! Johnny jumped in the water away from the oncoming disaster. By now I was almost there, but there was nothing I could do. The boat landed safely on the other side, without damage to the dock, the boat, or to people. A few onlookers came over to make sure everything was ok. For some strange reason, when the lake opened for public use, that particular dock sat fairly close to the water. The powers that be, raised the dock level after that incident. A major lesson was learned that day about starting in neutral! We hopped in the boat and took off across the lake. When we got out of sight of the dock, we stopped and caught our breath. Then we just laughed!! There was no need to share this escapade with Mom, we all agreed.

"June Bug" served us well and we traded for a bigger/better boat later.

Thanks for the memories,
Danny

10

Typical Family Travel in the '50s

This story is intended to document how the average family traveled in the '50s, for weekend road trips as well as annual vacations, when possible. Many families back then earned 2 weeks, sometimes more, of paid vacation. In addition, many of those dads were WWII Vets and wanted their families to see and experience a bigger view of the world as they had been able to, even during wartime conflict. It was a different time in our country especially as it relates to family mobility. Car travel was more prevalent than ever. It was the time of cute little family-owned motels, station wagons, and 20-cent gas! Airline travel was almost non-existent for average families. My dad flew related to business for Chance Vought, as did many, but certainly not for pleasure with the family! The net result was that trains were too slow, airlines were too expensive, and even without Interstate Highways, cars were the logical travel choice, even though most had no air conditioning in the '50s.

Now, this may be hard for grandkids to imagine, but there was no internet in those days. There were no laptops, tablets, no cell phones, no satellite radio, no ear pods, no nothing! Cars of that time typically were equipped with AM radios which would only pick up local stations. FM radios in cars weren't prevalent until the mid-sixties, however, Chrysler brands offered a built-in phonograph in the late sixties. But, we did have books, drawing tablets, toys, and limited games like I Spy; Rock/Paper/Scissors; The Alphabet Game; and 20 Questions. And, we mustn't forget, Burma Shave billboards! Ok, you got the picture, we had to entertain ourselves! However, we did have Stuckey's with their souvenirs and homemade pecan logs and of course other roadside special attractions such as reptile farms, caverns, and points of interest.

It should also be noted that cars of the day had full-width bench seats, front, and back. Now, unless you were an only child, the back seat was a literal war zone. There were constant sibling encroachment infractions. After ample warnings, my dad's arm seemed to grow by at least a foot to be able to give Johnny and/or me a "pop" to remind us to behave! I almost always sat behind my dad to avoid the long arm of the law! I our family we eventually evolved to a line defined by masking tape on the seat! Finally, Jan got older and could sit in the back seat with Johnny! I got to sit next to my dad and help him drive! On occasion, he'd let me shift the 3 on the tree! Sometimes he'd let me pretend to steer but always I'd let him support his right leg against my left, on those long stretches of highway. It probably didn't help him that much but it made me feel like I was helping him.

Then, when the family tired of the typical car games or maybe got sleepy, he and I would begin our favorite motoring game. We, very creatively, called it "Car Review". It began by calling out the make and Year, then evolved to naming the model, and then on to engine I.D. when specific emblems would allow. Discussions would follow about the vehicles we saw. Dad's favorites included Pontiacs with the lit-up Chieftain hood emblem and the Buicks with their fender portholes. Mine were the Cadillacs with their tailfins and Dagmar bumpers as well as the Mercurys with their big M emblems. My dad played to entertain me but I know he enjoyed it too.

Time passed quickly and those days were gone. But, it was fun while it lasted!

Thanks, Dad,
Danny

11

The Go-Devil Experiment

1956, 5th grade, West Side School
Arlington, Texas

It was the winter of 1956. I was in the 5th grade at West Side School. My family had a home on University Drive, southwest of Arlington State College, and within walking distance. University Drive splits Varsity Circle right down the middle, east to west. My Dad designed the house and actually played a part in building it in 1952. It was a modest two-bedroom, one-bath home with a single-car garage. Shortly thereafter we added another bedroom and bath. We had a great neighborhood with wonderful neighbors and lots of friends nearby. As a bonus, we had Doctor Wallace right next door and our preacher, John Shell, less than a hundred yards away. At our house, we subscribed to three magazines: Life; Southern Living; and Mechanix Illustrated. To this 11-year-old boy, the latter was the hands-down favorite. There were monthly car review articles by Tom McCahill, the ultimate authority on new car models and tests as well as several DIY projects. In the November issue, Uncle Tom, as he was known, reviewed the 1956 Chrysler 300B. This model sported 355 horsepower from a 354 cubic inch Hemi engine. More than one horsepower per cubic inch! Unheard of at that time. The 300 had dual four-barrel carburetors, dual exhausts, and a hot camshaft. It was the highest-performance American car of the time. Tom loved it and I loved the article.

In the same issue was a DIY, motorized, propel unit for an average bicycle. Just the thing for an 11-year-old boy! The name of the unit was "Go-Devil". Essentially it was a pusher trailer for a bike. It had a typical Briggs and Stratton lawnmower engine mounted on a platform with wheels. The engine had a centrifugal clutch, a belt drive to a reduction jackshaft with a sprocket output. The sprocket output was connected to the trailer wheel sprocket via a chain. The trailer unit pushed the bike through a flex connection to the seat post so the bike could lean in turns and the "Go-Devil" could stay flat. The speed was controlled with a pull cable throttle mounted under the bike seat easily operated with the right hand. Of course, I loved the thought of it and worked hard to convince my Dad to build it for me, with Mom's blessing of course. Amazingly, and with a few concessions, my Dad and I blew it by Mom. Hallelujah! We went to work and scavenged most of the components from an old reel lawnmower.

In a couple of weekends the "Go-Devil" was ready for a test run. Dad tried it first, for safety of course, then turned it over to me. I was excited, my first motor vehicle! I took off and as soon as I got out of site from Dad, I took it to full throttle! It would go about 20 MPH, flat out. What was cool was that it could push me 20 uphill or down. If I turned the bike to make a counterclockwise, tight circle, the "Go-Devil" could spin the inner wheel and lay down rubber donuts!! What a trip! The little unit was very dependable and lasted for quite some time. I finally wore it out and I moved on to other motorized adventures.

Needless to say, I was a popular kid at school the next day, and even 'til now, I've never seen another.

Thanks,
Danny

12

The Jet Roller Rink

Arlington, Texas
Circa 1956

It was the spring of 1957 and Arlington Texas had just gotten its first roller rink, "The Jet". We got GM in 1953, thanks to Tommy Vandergriff, but roller rinks were a lower priority! We were successful in 1956! It was a new, beautiful (at least to yours truly) building on west Norwood Lane, nearly to Bowen Road, on the south side of the street. It was a large building, about 150' by 100'. It had a wonderful, inviting, oak floor in the skating area. Like all rinks of the era, the designated direction was counterclockwise. The NASCAR guys must have been influential regarding that decision! HaHa!!

The front part of the rink was for the offices, the concession area, the skate rentals, and the restrooms. It was an absolute SKATER'S PALACE for Arlington! If you can't tell, this boy was pumped! Not only was it an incredible venue for fun, but also an opportunity to meet new girls! Now, some of these girls were from exotic places like Pantego, Johnson Station, Handley, Eastern Hills, Poly, Dalworthington Gardens, and even Grand Prairie! Of course, the local girls were usually the most friendly! And, as added bonus for the guys, some of the girls even had cute little skating outfits!

We had special skating sessions such as All Skate; Couples Only (now this was intended to be boys and girls back then); Reverse Skate (going clockwise); Backwards Skate; the Hokey Pokey; Speed Racing (my favorite), and others. The lighting effects during these events were absolutely awe-inspiring for those times. My goodness, for extra special effects, they even had a disco ball for romantic events! This was an awesome place, and I loved it!!

I was fortunate enough to live no more than two miles from "The Jet" and I could ride my bike there, which I did frequently! And as luck would have it, the Christmas before, Santa brought me the most wonderful present. Black leather Chicago roller skates with speed wheels, Dino bearings, and super performance toe stops! All packed in a superb pink and black hard case! I was in heaven! It was a great year!

Fun times in Arlington Texas!! Sweet Memories!
Danny

| 13 |

The Bronze Beauty

It was 1958 in Arlington, Texas. I was 13.

In Texas, at that time, kids could not drive legally until they were 15, UNLESS, we could muster up a "hardship" situation that would allow us to drive legally at 14. As hard as I tried, my parents would not fabricate a "hardship" excuse for me. They were right, unfortunately. That obstacle, however, opened up an opportunity for yours truly. Go-carts were a coming rage. There were tracks all over the metroplex. Somehow I managed to get a copy of an article in "The Reader's Digest" that concluded young go-cart drivers/racers actually made better auto drivers than those kids who didn't get that experience. Wow, talk about potent ammunition! I was loaded! I began to bring up that subject at the dinner table, and believe it or not, Billy and June were fairly receptive. I could not believe it!

So, one conversation led to another, and before you could say "Jack Robinson", we were at a local go-cart track watching a race. What a thrill for me. There was a track in Kennedale, another in Ft. Worth near the Trinity River, and another in Hurst, south of Bell Helicopter, in the river bottoms. The races were exciting, fun, and not too long. The people were friendly and nice. My work was almost done.

After a few weeks of negotiations (accommodations like washing dishes, mowing lawns, and washing cars), the deal was done. Now to find a cart. Mind you, these were not rental-style carts but racing carts capable of 50 MPH. We had met a man at an event at the track near Bell Helicopter. His name was Gene Apple, he was a Bell engineer and he had a nice bronze-colored cart for sale for $175.00. The "Bronze Beauty" had a 510 West Bend two-stroke with direct drive. She was a competitor and built for speed. That was a lot of money as real cars were readily available for that amount. Ok, we came to an agreed-upon price of $150.00. Man, that's a lot of washed dishes, car washings, and grass clippings!! Needless to say, I was tickled! We got her home and the fun began!

We went to a few races and I did OK, a couple of seconds and a third. It was obvious to me that all we lacked was power! Of course, my driving skills, or lack thereof, had nothing to do with it. At any rate, We disassembled the engine and discovered the ports could be opened a bit, the carb could be modified and the crankcase could be "stuffed". The latter is a rather sophisticated welding procedure only accomplished with "state of the art" equipment and welding talent far superior and far beyond the talents of your average ranch hand. Now that would have been a dilemma, EXCEPT, Billy worked at LTV and they had the most sophisticated equipment as well as the ultimate welders. And, he parked inside the gates! So one day he walked the crankcase in and back out the same day, "stuffed to the max". Thank you, Jimmy Ling, sir, the head of LTV!!

Once home, we put the engine back together. (Side note: you have to understand, my dad was mechanical, but about the time I was 12, he was handing the wrenches to me, instead of viceversa). Anyway, we got it together and the clearances were perfect. The welding experts really came through. On the track "Bronze Beauty" performed like " The Bronze Beast"! At least a 25% gain in power. No excuses now! We won a few races then baseball season started! The next future promised new thrills of cars, sports, and GIRLS!!

Great times and great memories!
Loved it!
Danny

╭──────────────╮
│   **14**   │
╰──────────────╯

The Sultans Car Club

Arlington, Texas
Circa 1959

Some of my friends and I were very lucky in 1959. We were a part of something unique, a church-sponsored car club, where none of the members had a driver's license or owned cars! We were 14-year-old boys with a very limited amount of knowledge about cars but also with a significant desire to learn more. That was us, The Sultans! And hey, we even had special window decals and embroidered white satin jackets! Our logo was a young, handsome Sultan speeding on a flying carpet equipped with a Hemi and straight pipes adding to the propulsion! Very tastefully presented of course. Our members were Jimmy D, Jack, David, Randy, Stewart, Steven, David, Jimmy H, Johnny, Gary, Dickie, John, Gene Scaggs (member/advisor), Floyd, Dennis, and Nicky.

It was an interesting time. Cars were very important to many young guys and they were improving at warp speed as the entire world was morphing faster than anyone could imagine. We were fortunate that some men of the church recognized the need and stepped up to the plate to help us youngsters navigate down the road. They secured a place for us to meet, generated meaningful programs, organized educational field trips and bonded with the group. Key sponsors were Vic Hart, Lloyd Counts, Herb Bloom and Bill Armstrong. Many other men helped as well along the way.

We were sponsored by The First Presbyterian Church in Arlington on South Collins just north of Park Row. Carter Junior High was just west of the church and Colonial Cafeteria was just south on Park Row. We met in an outbuilding designated as the Boy Scout Cabin. It was perfect for our little group. In our normal sessions we'd lock in on a particular system, like fuel delivery, valve timing and operation, exhaust, cooling, brakes, rear axle, transmissions, etc., but on occasion we'd need to have multiple sessions on one subject. We'd have guest presenters who were competent teachers of the subject matter. On one special occasion, we were able to visit the NHRA champion drag racer from Arlington, Vance Hunt. It was an awesome meeting. He took us into his shop and we saw the World Champion top fuel dragster up close and personal. He patiently explained how all the systems work together to propel the machine to the winner's circle. We were all blown away and grateful for his hospitality.

What a fun and educational time for us young guys. I think the men actually enjoyed sessions almost as much as we did. They went out of their way to help us and, I am grateful, as well I'm sure are the rest of the guys. Fun times for young teenagers! Thanks to all who took the time and energy to make that happen for "The Sultans"!

Fun memories,
Danny

15

Seeing Stars in 1959

It was the early fall of 1959 in Arlington, Texas. I was fortunate enough to be barely competent enough to be included on the 9th grade Ousley Rams football team. It was the beginning of a new season and we were excited about the new season. We were in the ninth grade. We had the potential of a winning year with a lot of great players. We had Rusty, Roger, Dennis, Nicky, Jack, Jimmy H., Hank, Denny, Gary G., Randy, Tim, Stewart, Jimmy F., Dennis H., Tommy, Jimmy N., Ricky, Ronny, Joe, Gary Don, Andy, Gary H., another Gary H., Jim B., Larry and yours truly, (we also had a wonderful cheerleading team and many loyal fans including beautiful Texas girls). We were having tackling practice that day at our practice field at Ousley Junior High School. It was a goathead-infested empty lot at the corner of West Abram and South Cooper. It was a hot and humid day and we were all starting to feel it. Our great coaches Harold Hill, Weldon Wright, and O'Neil Harris were providing motivation and training for all of us. We were surely on our way to an incredibly successful season.

We were having tackling practice with the eighth-grade players that day. We were rotating players on each side of the offensive and defensive sides of the line. Your particular draw in such an event was random. I happened to be on the defense side that particular day. Just to note: I was a pass receiver, not a defensive hammer! However, this particular day, I was the designated tackler. Yeah!! When my rotation came up my tackling partner was Charles McAlpine. This dude was a menacing running back, at about 180 and 6' at the age of 14. He was a "home run king" in baseball and one of the fastest and most powerful backs in local football. I was really excited and concerned, for sure!

"Ready, hut, hut", coach Hill exclaimed. Ok, let's go, I thought, trying to positively motivate myself, as well as attempting to be confident. One, two, three, I hit him (or maybe I should say he hit me)! It was over, I was out, I saw stars: "California Dreamin'! In my brief and unconscious state, Kay King (FYI, Kay was a beautiful girl that was a year older and admired by many including yours truly) was hovering over me, and actually concerned! Then, I was awake! I jumped up and asked, "Coach, did I get him?" "No son, he got you". That day confirmed for me that I was not destined to be a defensive player. I would leave those duties to my buds Gary Don and Gary Harwell! Really, all in all, it was a great day with my teammates and Kay King!

Thanks for the memories!
Danny

16

Ousley 8th Grade Football Party/Dance

Fall of 1958, Arlington, Texas

The season had come to a close and it had been very success-ful. We had all learned a lot from our great coaches: Harold Hill, O'Neil Harris, and Weldon Wright. Our defense had gotten stronger, quicker, and more able to adapt to our opponents' offense. Gary Harwell was a monster linebacker. Gary Don Page was in transition from being a great running back to a superior cornerback. Our offense had gotten faster and more precise in our play execution. Rodger was coming into his own as a QB and our backfield was comprised of Rusty, Joe, Dennis, Nicky, and Jimmy H. We were "picking 'em up and laying 'um down"! We were "rockin' and rollin'". Our O-line was dominating with Andy Chambers at center Gary Hampton and Hank Gibbs at guards, and Stewart DeVore, Ricky Jaeger, and Tim Gillespie at tackles and they were clearing the way for the backfield. Even the receiving crew, including Dennis Haag, Ronny Coker, Tommy Carrico, Jim Bergin as well as yours truly, had dramatically improved. We had a memorable year.

One game I particularly remember, against a good Birdville team, on a Thursday evening, was at their field. It was easy to recall, as their field was known as a "smelly field". It seems that their field was fertilized with water from the sewage waste re-cycling plant. Sadly, it had rained the night before. Now, that made for an interesting "unpleasant atmosphere" for the evening. The aroma was overwhelming! It was actually an unfair advantage for them!

(A special author's note: Now, to be fair to Birdville, I do have fond memories of the Holiday Roller Rink there, but that's another story)!

We had just completed a successful drive and score. Now, we were on defense. We must have been ahead by a substantial margin as Coach Harris yelled "Armstrong, get in there you are right defensive end!" In my mind, I yelled, "Say what?" But in real time I responded "Yessir! So, I went in, a defensive end! Here we are, like Ray Nitchske, a defensive, uncontrolla-ble maniac! Yeah! Hike! The ball was snapped. I lunged to the left then broke around to the right, then straight to the QB! I actually sacked the unsuspecting dude. No one was more surprised than me! So, we won and it was my SINGLE play in the limelight, as a defensive player!

(Another special author's side note: my mom said she could always pick me out on the field because my uniform was always spotless and unsoiled. Not so much a compliment but a reality! That game I was Ray Nitchske for a play!! I can live with that! My uniform was soiled for once)!

Back to the party. We were all there, some with guests, some without. Now, our guests were pretty and cute girls. All the cheerleaders including Joyce, Jacque, Margaret, Pam, Barbara, Carolyn, and Maudie were there, as well as many oth-ers. One thing about Arlington, we had an abundance of cute girls! I think, maybe, Rusty had finally discovered Margaret and my guest was Ema Jane McFaddin. We were all visiting and consuming snacks and punch when the coaches and their wives came in. There was O'Neil Harris and his wife Elizabeth. Then there was Coach Hill and his wife, then there was Coach Wright and his wife Raquel (that is a fictitious name). Holy smokes!! Raquel was the most beautiful woman I had ever seen!! I was able to officially meet her and I thought I would choke. We actually had a dance and I thought I would faint, but, I made it through. So sad, the wrong time and the wrong place, and she was married to Coach Wright! Oh well, "California Dreaming", again.

We had a great time with a fun bunch of friends & cool coaches (and their wives)! Very nice!! Great memories!

Thanks,
Danny

17

Wood Shop, Ousley, 8th Grade

It was 1958 in Arlington, Texas. Mr. Paul Booher was our pre-scribed educator, and much more like a coach than a teacher. He taught us as much about piecing lumber together as he did about blending individuals into a team of workers when needed. I'm not certain, and I don't think many knew it, but I think this was one of those "by invitation only", pre-college classes available only to exceptionally gifted, 8th grade, superior students. Of course, yours truly was one of those exceptional students selected for this academic challenge. We had an exceptional group of students including Kent Adams; Billy Ayers; Darryl Barton; Mac Browning; Tommy Carrico; Don Coder; Jerald Cope; Rene DeMott; Mike Bradford; Jimmy Houston; Bob Rucker; Gary Mansell; Bill Matitjschk; James McCury; Wayne Moreland; John Morris; Garry McMichael; Jimmy Norwood; Gary Page; CB Pride, David Strange; Clifford Wallar; Jimmy Templeton; Rusty Workman; and yours truly. Yes, as you've likely concluded, we were an elite group!

In the first two weeks, we learned about the different woods and their granular composition. Oak was typically tight-grained and dense, while pine was open-grained and rather soft. Walnut, my favorite, was in-between and a beautiful dark chocolate color. We learned that the more open-grained the wood, the more receptive to staining it was. We also learned that steaming the wood would allow for forming curved shapes and that dowels could be used instead of screws for attaching wood pieces together. We learned about butt joints and mortise and tenon joints, and when you should use each one. At that point, we were beginning to feel like young carpenters.

Next, we began to learn the technical aspects of the machinery we had available to us in the wood shop and how to safely operate them. We had planers, band saws, drill presses, routers, table saws, lathes, and of course all sorts of hand tools. Naturally, Mr. Booher concentrated on the safety aspects of operating the different tools and equipment. To his credit, we all completed the course with the same number of fingers that we started with!

Mr. Booher knew Buck Buchanan, Curtis' dad, as well as Dewey Kilpatrick, both local home builders. They allowed us to have a field trip to one of their homes under construction. Mr. Buchanan's house was in the process of getting the foundation poured and Mr. Kilpatrick's house was being framed. We all had a great time watching the construction activity as the builders and Mr. Booher explained what the craftsmen were doing.

After the first few weeks of woodworking and safety orientation, it was time to pick our projects. One overzealous young woodworker wanted to build a roll-top desk. Three other optimists wanted to build gun cabinets and four others wanted to build end tables. Now, Mr. Booher was not a large or loud man but could get his point across very convincingly. He was also very aware of his students' extremely limited abilities. It did not take him long to reign in our class and bring us back to the realities of elementary woodworking and cutting boards and book ends! Personally, I had come to a reality check pushing me toward a really nice cutting board for Mom!

One of my favorite recollections of the wood shop was the smell of the wood being cut, planed, sometimes burnished, and even sanded. Different woods had different smells. My favorite was the smell of walnuts. It was like ginger snap cookies and barbecue sauce, blended together.

So, it was a fun class, we all kept our fingers and lots of moms loved their awesome cutting boards!

Thanks, Mr. Booher,
Danny

18

Mom's Ban on Scooters and Cycles

Motor scooters and cycles were forbidden at the Armstrong home in Arlington, Texas. The ban came with due cause. My mom, June, and her boyfriend, Billy, (her future husband and my dad) had taken a day trip to Galveston from Houston, where they were both high school students. Six of the kids went there together to have fun at the beach as well as many additional activities available. Galveston at that time was a tourist attraction and offered many forms of entertainment including rental motor scooters. The gang decided it would be fun to splurge for the rental scooters. Now June had been on a motorcycle before as her big brother Bob had one, however, driving one was a totally different thing. Fun was being had by all on the streets of Galveston. The riders changed places and now June was in front. In the blink of an eye, June ran into the back of a stopped, tan, '34 Ford Cabriolet. Oh no, there she was lying on the pavement with a bleeding, broken jaw. So much for that fun date! Her jaw was wired shut and she was on a liquid diet for six weeks. That little romance was likely put on hold for a while, at least as long as it took Billy to get back into good graces with June's mom, Pallie.

So, literally from that point on, my lot would be cast as a "scooterless son". This was an almost unbearable shame for a young gearhead. Of course, like any kid, I pushed as hard as possible for reconsideration, even promising things I could likely not deliver, all to no avail. As a consolation, when I was 11 or so, my dad and I talked June into letting us build a bike pusher trailer, with a lawnmower engine, called a "Go-Devil". After all, it wasn't a two-wheeled, motorized unit, but a four-wheeled, speed-limited, safe, lawnmower-powered, fun machine. One that father and son could bond together while building, was just an added benefit. It worked! Success! The "Go-Devil" would push my bike almost 20 MPH, uphill! It was the only one I ever saw. In grade school, at least in Arlington, I was the only kid with a powered bike.

Now, in eighth grade, we moved to Ousley Junior High, and a bunch of kids had scooters. There were Isettas, Vespas, Lambrettas, Sears Cruiseairs, Zimmers, and Cushman Highlanders and Eagles. The Mustang was truly a mini motor-cycle from England, that hit the scene in Arlington in about 1956. They had twice the horsepower of the most powerful Eagle and with one more gear. They would go an honest 80 MPH while the fastest Eagle, on a good day, downhill, could make 60. We had a couple of Mustangs at Ousley owned by Dick Carmichael and Robert Young. The Mustangs were the performers but the Eagles were the coolest! Bobby Cales had a black Eagle with dual pipes, shaved head, dual mirrors, and a custom leather seat with leather fringe. The pure, sweet sound of eight horsepower exiting from dual, straight pipes was mu-sic to my ears! It was the pinnacle of my desires, but not to be realized!

Over at Carter, there were lots of scooters as well. Jimmy Duppstadt had a Cruiseaire, Norman Roberts had a white Eagle, Bob Wood had a green Eagle and Glenn Hickson had a grey Highlander. Donny Lucas had a Black Eagle that was supposedly faster than any other Eagle in the area.

I had to accept the fact that it wasn't to be, I could not have an Eagle! Time passed. I was over it as cars were in.

Fast forward to 1968. Now that was a good year! New baby girl (Amy), new house, new car, AND, new motorcycle! It was a new Honda 350 Scrambler! Loved it! Since that time I've had no less than 15 motorcycles and scooters.

Fast forward to 2013. I had purchased a couple of antique Vespas, got them running, and had fun tooling around the neighborhood and giving the grandkids rides in the yard. I sold them and began looking for that special Eagle I had always wanted. I searched to no avail. Then, with the help of Ron Westendorf (Bobbie Allen's husband), I found her in Edmond, Oklahoma. She was a robin's egg blue, 1965 Super Silver Eagle with an electric start. The top of the heap! I cut the deal and picked her up in a trailer. I named her Baby Blue. Sweet day!

Enjoyed the ride,
Danny

Let's Play Catch!

The most simplistic connection.
Growing up in Arlington, Texas.

I can't express the incredible "connection" we have with another person when we simply play catch. Be it baseball or football, it is purely mindless, calming, and actual therapy. It can be with your brother, your mom, your sister, your dad, your friend, your uncle, or your grandfather, it's all good! Totally a simple activity with the freedom to express your best pitch or pass or catch without critique from outsiders.

It would be difficult to calculate the hours and the fun had while playing catch. With another kid, your conversation while doing so might be about anything, short of religion and politics, an early learned lesson! While playing with an adult it became more like practice or teaching, as they were trying to help you improve, but it was still fun.

I was fortunate enough to be able to enjoy those times with a couple of my grandparents, Fred, my Mom's dad, and Beryl, my Dad's mom. Not for too many years though as they were aging and I was growing. I do remember it though and had fun doing it. I'm reminded of many an afternoon, my bro

Johnny and I would wait for Dad to get home from work so we could pitch to him. Billy worked at LTV and got home at about 5:30. We lived in College Hills on University Drive. This was about 1959 so I was 14 and Johnny was 11. That was about the time I had to stop bullying him as he was getting too big and strong! Anyway, we both pitched for our respective, Arlington summertime ball teams. Johnny could throw exceptionally hard for his age and I could hold my own. We had purchased a nice catcher's mitt for Dad and he had built a pitcher's mound we could throw from. We would take turns throwing to Dad. Every once in a while one of us would throw an exceptionally fast ball and Dad would jump up from his catcher's position and holler! Of course, Johnny and I would laugh. Fun memories!

The most fun, however, was with a bud who had comparable skills. We'd pretend to catch like Mantle and throw like Feller. Oh, what games we won for our respective imaginary teams!! With football, touchdowns, and wins were prevalent! Mindless, bonding, and exercise to boot!! Catch!

Warm memories. Thanks to all my "catch" partners.
Danny

20

FFA Experience @ Ousley

1960 Ousley Jr. High School
Arlington, Texas

It seemed like a fun thing to do in 1960. I was just a kid looking for new and different things to experience. Future Farmers of America offered me that chance. After all, what could be more fun than castrating calves and milking cows?? And when a guy tired of those activities, other opportunities were presented in the form of sheep shearing, mucking cattle stalls at the Fort Worth Stock Show, and even calf birthing was optional for extra credit! Lucky for me, I didn't need that extra credit!

With sincerity, I must say it was a very rewarding experience, and I'm so glad to have done it. We had a great teacher, Mr. Bohannon. He really knew his, uh, excrement. He had kind of a "dry" approach to teaching but he was determined (and challenged) to actually teach us valuable lessons for our future. The entire year was like a continuous "ranching and farming" field trip. We learned very valuable lessons. These lessons included being certain to wash your hands, and arms, prior to assisting with calving, use sharp tools when cutting a calf, and, very importantly, warm your hands prior to starting to milk a cow. These were very important and useful lessons!

We learned about acres, fencing, and animal husbandry. Each student (and I use that term very loosely) had to have a project (a living animal) each semester. Most of the animals survived the term. Some of the guys already lived on a farm and had cows or horses, so that made it easy for them. Others, like me, lived in town and had to be a little more innovative. I asked, but dogs, cats or goldfish didn't count.

So, the first term I got a sheep. She was beautiful. I named her Shirley. What pretty eyes she had. I cared for her for several months-feeding, combing, cleaning, and watching her grow. Gee, she really filled out and what chops she had! She was warm and cuddly when she was young but as she aged she became more demanding. She weighed about 70 pounds when it was time to end the relationship. We took her to the Ft. Worth stockyards auction and I said goodbye. Parting is such sweet sorrow. I was finally free of her selfish ways. So long Shirley. She brought 35 cents a pound. What a deal, I would have given her away! My next term project was to raise 50 chicks. We built a small pen and I gave them their new home. They were tiny and cute when I got them but after feeding them mass quantities of food for 12 weeks or so, they had become insidious little monsters. It was time to emulate Colonel Sanders and turn them into chicken dinners. They were in a better place after all and everyone who savored them enjoyed their tenderness! I conclude it was due to the loving care they received from yours truly. I passed!

We had a great class of really diverse guys I likely wouldn't have gotten to know and befriend if not for this opportunity. We had Chester, Clarence, Bobby, Duane, Joey, Kenneth, Stanley, Tony, C.B., Ray, John, Olen, Hank, Johnny, Jerry and others. All in all, a great group of fun Future Farmers. I was lucky to be a part of this team.

What a fun ride!
Thanks guys & critters,
Danny

21

First Presbyterian Arlington Youth Group Trip to New Mexico & Ghost Ranch

Summer 1959

At The First Presbyterian Church in Arlington, we were blessed to have a few extraordinary couples to be our youth group sponsors, and I was fortunate enough to come along at the right time to be a recipient. The youth group consisted of teenagers who were pre-high school ages. Our sponsors were the Willmanns, Charlie, and Patty. They lived near the Church on McKay Street. Charlie was the manager at the Sears store out on East Abram. He resembled Dean Martin in his looks and mannerisms. We teased him relentlessly but I think he actually enjoyed it! Patty was a homemaker and an organizer. She was the worker! They had two sons, Chuck, a year behind me, and Dan, a couple of years younger than Chuck. Then we had the Farrells, Don and Betty. They lived on West Cedar near Randol Mill and Davis. Don was a veterinarian and an Aggie. He and Dad were tight. Don and Betty were five and ten years younger than my parents, respectively. Don was funny but dry; Betty was energetic and vivacious. They were wonderful people and had two sons, Mark was six years younger than me and Eddy was two years younger than Mark. Anyway, these couples would open their homes up to our group, feed us supper, lead somewhat of a religious/learning session, and then lead us in discussions that were meaningful to us at that time. Things like: "sexual identity", " critical race theory" and "the fairness of boys competing as girls against girls"! Seriously, we discussed dating the opposite sex, movies, and getting along with family. Really! Somehow, that seemed important the time!

These two families, along with the Harts, the Crawfords, the Garrisons, the Heitts, the Armstrongs, and several others, were an integral part of a subset of The First Presbyterian Church membership called "The Mariners". These families truly played a significant part in the raising of all of us lucky kids, really like an extended church family. The Mariners went on annual retreats, appropriately named cruises, to meet with other Mariners groups from around the country, always at a location of interest and seemingly quite affordable. Quite a unique "brotherhood/sisterhood/familyhood" of fellow Presbyterians. It seemed that we always went north and east as there must not have been many Presbyterians out west. Go figure! There were kid activities and adult activities, truly fun trips for all!

Back to the story. So the Farrells the Crawfords and the Willmanns took on the challenge of taking a group of 13-15-year-old kids on a mobile retreat reaching all the way to Farmington, NM, and back. Along the way, we saw Palo Dura Canyon, a Native Indian Pueblo, the beginnings of the Rio Grande River, Taos, and Ghost Ranch. There were about five guys including John Donaghy, Jimmy Houston, Chuck

Willmann, Eddie Knight, and me. There were about five girls including Harriett Morgan, Janice Luttrell, Pat Hurley, and the Heitt twins, Jean and Janet. We also had a senior sponsor, Carol Ann Snider, accompany us as a younger chaperone. She was about 17 at the time and was a great addition to our group. Churches along the way would host us with a dinner and some entertainment. The youth from the local church would be there to greet us and to socialize. When there was a piano in the house, Jimmy Houston would "wow" us all with his ability to play "boogie woogie". He was phenomenal! On most occasions, we'd bed down in our bedrolls on the floor of their activities room. All were super cordial and welcoming congregations! I think it costs our families about $100.00 per kid. It was a very economical expedition and must have been underwritten by sponsors.

Some evenings we would camp out with a small fire, roasting hot dogs and finishing up with s'mores! Dr. Farrell would always finish those outdoor meals with a cigar. One, and only one, evening us guys talked Don into letting us have cigars as well (after all, we were almost men, uh-huh). Well, after about 10 minutes of aggressive puffing, the urge to upchuck hit us all! While we all were hurling we could hear Don snickering in the background. None of us ever bugged him the balance of the trip about allowing us to partake in the after-dinner cigar ritual!! Torturing us, he would offer, but we would all decline.

Our furthest stop was in Farmington, NM, way up in the northwest corner of the state. The host church was the First Presbyterian Church of Farmington. The welcoming group was very nice and accommodating. However, there was an immediate and interesting problem for me. Of the youth there to welcome us, there was this girl. She was about 5'4", slim, red-headed, with a light freckle faced, an absolutely gorgeous girl. She wore a cute orange and yellow sun dress. Striking, to say the least! She certainly had my attention! When the meal was finished they had music for us kids to dance and it didn't take me long to work my way closer to this New Mexico "Goddess". Her name was Janet Tucker. Her dad was an Elder in the church. We danced a bit then sat down and we began to visit. Funny, she seemed as interested in me as I was in her. We hit it off, to say the least. We talked for a long time then we had a couple more dances and I thought "This is it, she's the one!". We talked for another hour or so, then our last dance was to Johnny Mathis' " It's Not For Me To Say". I was smitten. It was hard to come to the realization that we had to head for home the next morning. As we were pulling out of the church parking lot, a few of the church members had gathered to give us a warm sendoff. Many were there but I could see only one. You guessed it! It's needless to say, but I was mentally occupied the entire way home. But it was not to be. We wrote a few letters back and forth, then the letters stopped. It was a sad time for me.

It was a great 10-day adventure and we were so fortunate our sponsors were willing to take us. We were able to meet a lot of new friends and see places we hadn't seen before, as well as grow closer to all our participants. No one got hurt, or sick (save the cigar ordeal), nor got their feelings stepped on! A successful trip by anyone's standards!

Thanks to all that made it happen,
Danny

22

Donuts

It was 1957 in Arlington, Texas, and donuts
on Sundays were an enjoyed luxury!

The First Presbyterian Church had recently moved to their new campus on South Collins. Commercial development was strong and bustling all up and down East Park Row. As a part of that growth, a new Page's Rexall Drug store was part of a new strip center on the northeast corner of East Park Row and South Collins. Harry Lawing's newly located Texaco station and a new 7/11 were on the immediate corner and the strip center was situated behind them. In the strip center, there were other businesses such as a grocery store, a fabric store, a dry cleaner, and others. This story centers around the drugstore.

Page's was a big drugstore at that point in time. It happened to be large enough that it included a full-service soda fountain/restaurant in the back corner of the store. There were booths and a bar with stools for folks to enjoy their offerings of breakfast, burgers, sandwiches, and of course, milkshakes and malts. Another item they offered for morning fare was freshly made donuts, served hot, with butter.

Our Sunday school started at 9:30 at First Pres, and lasted about an hour, then church services started at 11:00. In 1957 none of my friends had their own cars yet but Page's was only a few hundred yards away, therefore, we could walk there for a little snack before church services started. I remember the first time we ventured there between services. My buds Jimmy Houston, John Donaghy, Johnny Blesi, Stephen Hart, Linda Moore, Jacque Deering, Joyce Heffington, Cindy Crayton and Harriett Morgan all went along. Our waitress was named Louise and she was very nice to us kids. The donuts were a nickel each. We all ordered two apiece. We all asked for them warm, with butter. In a few minutes, Louise brought them out on little plates and the smell was to die for. Then we all dug in! Now I had certainly had donuts before theirs and hundreds of them later, but none can compare to those!! Our little trips to Page's became a regular event and Louise was always glad to see us every Sunday morning for at least a couple of years! To this day, that is my favorite way to eat donuts!

Thanks, Louise,
Danny

Model Trains

A lifelong fascination for an Arlington kid.

In assessing my personal addiction, I've concluded there are several contributing factors. They are as follows:

First: the times. Almost all of us early "baby boomer" kids growing up in the '40s and '50s, were exposed to real trains, many of which were utilizing steam locomotives. These steam locomotives were still in use even though they were being replaced by the evolution of diesel/electric locomotives. The "steamers" were huge engines with monstrous wheels and exposed pushrods and cylinders, visually mesmerizing all lookers-on. They were almost alive, pulsing and breathing pieces of history, literally unchanged for 150 years, at that time. They literally industrialized our country. They had steam whistles and were operated by engineers, easily visible in the cab. They had numbers like "Engine #9" and names like "The Wabash Cannonball" and sometimes were in the movies! They had charisma and personalities. Many a youngster had aspirations and dreams of being an engineer, rolling down the tracks! The diesels had streamlining and pretty paint jobs but somehow, not quite the same appeal. On many occasions a couple of friends would ride their bikes with me down to the Davis Drive crossing and wait for passing trains. We'd place pennies on the tracks and wait for them to be smashed by the wheels. Sometimes the engineers would wave to us and blow the whistle. Good times.

Second: the product. After WWII ended, our young men were returning and they were starting families. The US economy was booming as good jobs were abound. Retailers around the country were working overtime and their cash registers were smoking hot. The US model train manufacturers were setting sales records and the market consisted of Marx, American Flyer (owned by Gilbert the maker of Erector Sets), and Lionel. Marx was sort of the entry level train set with American Flyer next, then Lionel at the top of the heap with more models and accessories than the others combined.

Note: Lionel was founded by Joshua Lionel Cowen in 1900.
Note: American Flyer sold its first electric train in 1918.
Note: Marx electric trains were first available in 1919.

Third: the marketing. By the early '50s the model train companies had elaborate catalogs and a host of retailers. Lionel seemed to partner with the largest retailers, then American Flyer, then Marx. There weren't any Arlington hobby shops in the early '50s yet so we had to go to Fort Worth to see much in the way of model trains. My first recollection of laying eyes on a significant layout and a multitude of engines, cars and accessories was Christmas time in 1952 in downtown Fort Worth at Leonard Brothers on Main Street. The Lionel display in the basement was magnificent! There were freight trains pulled by steamers and passenger trains pulled by streamlined diesels. There were bridges and switches as well as cattle loading pens, milk loading cars, sawmills and water towers. I was in heaven! There were huge transformers with throttle handles on each end! I watched the trains operate as long as Mom would let me.

The nice man operating the trains gave me a catalog and wished me Merry Christmas as we left. Back home I studied that catalog and wished for one of every item. Marketing accomplished, they sure had this boy! OK, those were the driving factors.

I got my first train set for Christmas in 1953. It was a starter freight set from American Flyer. Dad helped me set it up around the Christmas tree in the living room. What a feeling! Controlling my own train, all be it in circles around the tree! That Christmas, my little bro Johnny, got some Lincoln Logs and some G.I. Joe figurines. We built little forts across the tracks with soldiers inside, then smashed into them with the train going full speed. Great fun! As Christmases and birthdays passed I accumulated more track, switches, and cars. Then, after a couple of years, interests changed and the trains remained boxed up. Over the next few years I visited several of the neighborhood kids with train sets and enjoyed them but I never knew anyone with a permanent layout over those years. I thought that was what I eventually wanted someday, somewhat like what I experienced at Leonard Brothers.

The train bug returned in 1978 and I built an elaborate, two level, 'N' gauge, permanent layout in half our garage at our home in Woodland Park. I had 47 engines and 190 cars. With multiple transformers I could run seven trains at one time. It was a little too tiny for kids to operate and enjoy.

The Lionel "flu" hit in the '80s and I sold all the 'N' gauge equipment and physical layout and evolved to the Lionel 'O' gauge trains. The layout I built was a multi-level, garage and a half size set up, in many ways like the set I'd seen at Leonard Brothers in 1952. I had most of the accessories and could run multiple trains a once. Family and friends really liked it as it brought back fond childhood memories.

When we moved to Kennedale in '93, I now had a 30' x 40' metal shop in the back. The Lionel layout grew to take up most of the building. Now my grandkids could help me with new additions and operations. I had accumulated about 60 engines and close to 250 cars. One passenger set, the Santa Fe, had a length exceeding 15'. The layout had 48 switches, four transformers and accessories galore. The wiring job was immense with over two miles of wire under the layout. Lots of fun was had in that shop with grandkids and friends.

Now that we live in Santa Fe, the bug is beginning to bite again! We'll see!

Thanks Mr. Lionel Cowen,
Danny

24

Road Trips

*Road trips of the '50s and early '60s were made so much more
fun by the small sign messages from Burma Shave.*

Burma Shave was a prominent, American, brushless, shaving cream company that had an interesting advertising medium in the form of a series (4-8) of small sequential billboards, about 1'x3', placed on private land, just inside the property line along the highway. The signs were about 100' apart so you would read one, then the next. Typically, the signs were red and white or orange and black with all-caps lettering. They told a humorous little tale always ending in "Burma Shave". They used them from the 1920s until 1963, when they were deemed to be a liability for the company as cars were going faster, and reading the signs might make a driver lose concentration.

Company example #1: YOUR SHAVING BRUSH/ HAS HAD IT'S DAY/ SO WHY NOT/ SHAVE THE MODERN WAY/ WITH BURMA SHAVE

Company example #2: HARDLY A DRIVER/ IS NOW ALIVE/ WHO PASSED ON HILLS/ AT 75/ BURMA SHAVE

Dan's Example #1: There once were two sisters from Alice/ they were to visit their cousins in Dallas/ they were rapidly approaching an upcoming curve/ and weren't aware of how tight it was/ into the pasture they went/ without broken bones or even a dent/ So don't be reckless, please slow down/ then you can be seen in the next Texas town!/ Smooth on the curves/ Burma Shave!

Dan's Example #2: Slow down your pace/ put on a happy face/highways aren't for rage/ be around to turn the next page/ smooth and easy/ Burma Shave!

We sure enjoyed those little billboards! Bet you did, too.

Thanks, Burma Shave,
Danny

25

Arlington Theater, 1950–1974

What a wonderful escape and a memorable place for many a young Arlingtonite! The theater opened in early 1950 with the showing of "The Story of Seabiscuit" starring Shirley Temple and closed in 1974 with "The Absent-Minded Professor" starring Fred MacMurray. It was located on the west side of North Center, just south of the Division Street intersection. It was a beautiful, two-level, 1200-seat auditorium. To a six-year-old in 1951, there to watch Alice in Wonderland, it was an awesome place! There was a balcony and an amazing concession stand. Back then the admission was a dime and popcorn or a candy bar was only a nickel. My first recollection of a manager/owner was Mr. Eppes. He had two sons who helped him at the theater a little later. Bubba was a couple of years older than me and Sid was a couple of years younger. In 1994 the theater became Johnnie High's Country Music Review.

Arlington Theater was a wonderful addition to a growing little college town and the entire population enjoyed it, especially us younger folks. By the time I was 12, my buds and I could go, unchaperoned, and we loved westerns. Now, it just so happened that our town ambassador, Marshall, absolutely loved westerns, as well. On multiple occasions, in the middle of a heated chase, with the bad guys going after the good guys, at the most tense moment, Marshall would jump up out of his seat and yell "Watch out, they're behind you"! It became a regular occurrence and we came to, if not expect it, go ahead and enjoy it. If it made Marshall happy, it made us happy!

I think this was a matinee-only occurrence, but Mr. Eppes was known to stop the projector, walk out on the stage, and instruct the rambunctious audience to calm down and respect the other viewers. Only then did he restart the projector.

What a great place! What great memories! Lots of fun times, especially in the balcony! I suspect you have some special memories of your own.

Thank you, Mr. Eppes,
Danny

Santa's Ride, Circa 1956

BY DANNY ARMSTRONG

'Twas Christmas Eve and Santa was flustered.
On HIS night of the year, his deer couldn't muster.

The reindeer were sick, as a virus had spread!
They were cursed with fever, and aches in their head.

Intestinal problems at the pole did abound,
so they stayed in their stalls, with illness all around.

Santa was worried they wouldn't make the border.
Even if they did, it would be a messy disorder.

Santa's sled was more loaded than ever,
So the power required was quite an endeavor.

His sleigh was loaded with toys all around.
How could it ever get off of the ground?
Trains were for Johnny and dolls meant for Bonny.
Toy guns for Ronny and a new bike for Lonny.
Trucks aimed for Royce and skates set for Joyce.

Toy rockets for Jimmy and a doll house for Ginny.
A doctor's kit for Tommy and a toy pony for Connie.
Books for Becky and a ball bat for Nicky.
A puppy for Jane, Lincoln Logs for Wayne.
A toy car for Dan, a toy flute for Jan.
A suitcase for Linda and a diary for Brenda!
It was a loaded sleigh! Needless to say!

But his power source had failed, he needed another,
One he could count on through all kinds of weather.
Powerful yet steady! Strong as an Ox.
A good choice was needed, shrewd as a fox!

Now Santa had an awesome collection of cars,
Which was very well-known both near and far.
He had 'Vettes and Hemis and Panchos and Cammers.
He had Tri-Powers, Firedomes, and even Cross-Rammers!

Santa had tough choices for his engine direction,
But a bored Merc "Flattie" was his final selection!

The elves got busy and made the swap,
with time to spare, they put a blower on top!

They linked up the turbines and added small wings,
Then they cranked her up, to hear "Flattie" sing.

Around the world, the "Flattie" performed to a tee,
Bringing kids everywhere their Christmas glee!

So all was well in '56,
The "Flattie" saved Christmas, and no one got sticks.

Across the lands and back to the pole,
Santa was joyous and let the world show.
In his farewell, he exclaimed for all to know
"The Flathead was still king, let the cheers flow"!

Merry Christmas!
Danny

27

The "Neighborhoods" of Arlington

During the '50s and '60s

PRELUDE: Did you ever notice that street names for most towns had a rather simple "set" of parameters used by most city councils. That "set" of acceptable names was fairly limited but almost universally used. Typically, names that include hills, valleys, views, and meadows seem to be grossly exaggerated. OK enough already!

Our Arlington forefathers were no exception when it came to naming streets. We were a normal town with a Center, Main, all the geographical directions, many numerals as well as names of the founders of the community. Heck, at one time I thought of acquiring a lot on the corner of East North Street and North West Street, in Arlington for a business. I just couldn't come around to doing it. I could visualize giving directions over the phone and how confusing it would be to the potential customer! Ok, please pardon me, back to the storyline.

In Arlington, we had many great neighborhoods. Those names that developers use to describe a portion of land with their "signature" on it, got sort of lost over a period of 70 years or so. I can recall some neighborhood names and certainly many streets, but most of the descriptive development names elude me. Almost all of the larger neighborhood names came about during the population explosion after WWII and beyond. You can likely remember yours but not many more, I sure can't. Prior to WWII, Arlington wasn't large enough, nor did it have many large land developers, consequently neighborhoods simply took on the name of a nearby landmark or had no name at all.

In the '50s and '60s, growing Arlington had Parkview Estates, a nice neighborhood off East Abram, across from the Bull Pen Drive-In. We had Happiness Homes off South Collins near Blanton. There was Meadow Oaks Estates off South Collins just north of Mitchell, as well as Bluebonnet Hills which was just west of South Davis School. Southwood Estates was south of Park Row off South Davis, and Cedar Springs Estates was just east of Collins off Mitchell. A little later, other neighborhoods included: The Oaks; Woodland West; Briarwood; Shady Valley Estates; Interlochen; Mill Creek Estates; Shorewood Estates; Sherwood Estates; Parkwood Hills, Lakewood; and Bever Estates, a neighborhood that was an absolute incubator for cute girls coming of age. There was Alice Venom, the Duckett sisters, Jan Clements, the Scanlon sisters, the Pilcher sisters, and DeeDee Mosely. There were many other neighborhoods I just simply can't recall their names.

Our particular neighborhood was called College Hills and consisted of Varsity Circle and University Drive. Nearby streets were Shady Lane, West Second, West Fourth, Kirby, Summit, and South Davis. We were close enough to Arlington State College that my dad could walk to work. Our address was 210 University, right in the center of the circle, at the top of the small hill.

Our neighbors were: Dr. Frank and Nancy Wallace and their three girls, Wendy, Cathy, and Muffie to the east; then the Waggoners with their kids Mike and Gay on the corner. West there was Charles and Virginia Brown and their two girls Becky and Nancy, then the Tingleys, then next to them, Marcus and Wynelle Huebner and their family including Richard and Roger (the twins), Mary, Taylor, Leah, and Nell. Across the street, we had the Stanleys, and going west were the Garnetts, Coop, and Louise Cooper and their kids, Scott, Jeff, and Sarah. Then the McCalls, then the Mazos, Larry and Dougey. Going east across the street were the Walkers, the Challengers, and the mystery neighbor (?).

We were among the first to build there in 1952. We were renting a house very nearby, on West Fourth, so we could go by and check the progress every few days, after quitting time of course. I was very excited the day the stack of lumber was delivered. It was fun watching it being built. The neighborhood was a mix of smaller, frame homes built on one lot, like ours, to larger, brick homes built on two lots. Watching the builders was always entertaining to me as well as trying to figure out the final floor plan with only the foundation or framework to go by.

Varsity Circle was fairly large and was comprised of 66 families. Including University Drive families, the immediate neighborhood was 81 homes, and about half of them belonged to my friends including Tommy Snyder; Pat Arlington; Carol Stanford; Phillip Wilbur; Jan Johnson; Johnny Blesi; Bill Sutherland; Brad Wileman; Judy Ball; Jeannie Shell; the Justice twins; Roger Adams; Ingrid Breazeale; Jack Merbler; Linda Moore; Jerri Tucker; Stewart DeVore; the O'Dells; the Yates; the Lees; the Swaffords; the Kilpatricks; the McCoys, the Jenkins, the Howard's, the Peterson family and several others. Not far away we're the Baileys, the Hightowers, the Meiers, the Murchisons, the Shupees, the Roberts, the Mahans, the Smiths, the Boones, the Tinkers, the Scotts, the Harts, and the Godfreys. We even had Mrs. Gregory the piano teacher. Varsity Circle was about a mile around and I must have ridden it a thousand times over the 10-year period we lived there, on my bike or other forms of "kid" transportation. Just riding around the block I could always find a friend or two to stop and play catch, or basketball, or football with, any time of year! The neighborhood families were very supportive of all the kids and their social fundraisers. College Hills was a wonderful place to grow up. We had a creek where we could fish for crawdads, a nice park with playground equipment and a baseball diamond, a lake behind Philip Wilbur's house, and a spooky baby graveyard and chapel called the Berachah Cemetery near the little lake. It was part of, what used to be in the early 1900's to about 1935, a home for erring and outcast girls. It seemed especially scary at Halloween time!! An added bonus was that we had Mr. Farhat's "Chuck's Cafe" just five minutes away on South Davis! Mr. Farhat and his family were always exceptionally nice to us neighborhood kids. Many family friendships were formed and lasted well beyond local and distant relocations. We were all blessed to be able to enjoy such wonderful experiences at that time of our lives!

Thanks for the neighborhood memories,
Danny

28

Austin Patio Dude Ranch

Grapevine, Texas, circa 1956

For some reason that I will never understand, many 10 to 14-year-old girls are infatuated with horses. What is it?? They are big, and powerful, require a ton of care and maintenance and expense, they get sick, their stalls have to be cleaned, they need tons of food, and they may, or likely not, show any affection or appreciation. They sometimes bite your legs and sometimes toss you off for no apparent reason. They may go left when you want them to go right! They may go fast when you want them to go slow. They never imply they are sorry and never seemingly ask for your forgiveness. Generally, they are messy and cause a lot of trouble! And talk about flatulence superiority, no contest! OK, I've got it!! In essence, the girls were learning how to deal with their future boyfriends or husbands. Good training, if you ask me!!

So, in the defined timeframe, there were a lot of birthday parties held at The Austin Patio Dude Ranch in Grapevine. It was located at, what is now, the north end of the DFW runways, at the precise location of the Bass Pro Shop! It was a beautiful 100-acre site with lots of horse trails, beautiful oak trees, and a party/patio area with tables and entertainment areas. I was fortunate enough to be a guest at several of these parties. The parties were hosted by Jane, Suzanne, Carolyn, and Joyce, among others. Initially, upon arrival, each guest was assigned a particular horse, supposedly somewhat matched to their "horsemanship" abilities. Now, just to be clear, I never overstated my horse-related abilities; however, I was assigned to "Nasty Nancy". Nice name, I thought to myself. Each kid got their own particular horse. I looked around and all the kids seemed very comfortable. Nancy and I were pretty friendly at first, but then I could sense it, she misinterpreted my intentions! Our guide/host, Dustin, began our trail ride through the property and we started pretty slow. What a nice, controlled pace, I told myself.

Bad read on my part! As Dustin got us going a little faster down the trails, "Nasty Nancy" began to show her "true Nastiness", as she bolted forward, with no regard to low-hanging oak branches. It was obvious, even to me, that she wanted me on the ground! Well, I knew I was in trouble! I started softly talking to her. "Nancy, you are the prettiest girl here, you are the sweetest and most desirable girl I know. I truly love you, and only you !" She calmed down in just a minute, and was very submissive! She and I had a great understanding from that point on. I fed her, I brushed her, I washed her, I brought her carrots. Anytime I was invited back to Austin Patio Ranch for another party, I always requested "Nasty Nancy"! And hey, she wanted me! What a girl!

What a grand memory!
Thanks,
Danny

29

Restaurants We Could Choose From

Pre-1966 in Arlington
(Note: I didn't include eating places that you could not
be seated in, nor did I include soda fountains.)

Like most families in Arlington in the 1950s, we didn't eat out a lot. After-church lunches were not uncommon on Sundays, but other eat-out dinners during the week were uncommon. Sometimes, burgers out during the week were not out of the question, but It was a very special occasion when we went out for a sit-down dinner during the week. Rarely would we go to Fort Worth, and even more rare, Dallas, for a nice meal. Now mind you, this was pre 1963 and we were a male-dominated family. It's my feeling that families which happened to be female-dominated cared more for the fancy dinners than we did. Like most boys, quantity and speed were more important related to meals, than quality, ambiance and fancy settings. Now, sometimes, my mom and dad would go to those places without us anxious kids and we were delighted NOT to go!

Maybe once or twice a month, after church, we'd go to Wyatt's Cafeteria on East Abram or after it was built, Colonial

Cafeteria on East Park Row. Johnny and I had a budget of $1.25 each for our trays of food. Back then you could fill the tray for that, excepting a fancy desert. If we exceeded our allocation we had to pay Dad out of our allowance. I remember the liver and onions with cream gravy, the creamed spinach, and the Ritz Cracker pie being exceptional at Wyatt's.

Then, maybe twice a month on Fridays, we'd go to one our favorite other places. If Mexican food was the family choice, we'd go to LaTapatia, on West Division at North West Street. It was a two story building with living quarters upstairs and dining and kitchen downstairs. I think two sisters owned and ran the restaurant and lived upstairs. We thought the food was great, especially the cheese enchiladas, the guacamole tostadas, and for the finale, fresh pecan pralines! For a change we'd go to LaCasita Mexican restaurant out on West Division but it was not usually first choice. It later became Catfish Sam's. Into the '60s we began to frequent a Fort Worth favorite, Joe T. Garcia's, off of North Main. It was authentic Tex-Mex and was always busy. When we first started eating there they only had about ten tables in the little house on the front corner. All told, I'd bet I've been there at least 200 times. Consistently good!

Another favorite was Arlington Steak House on West Division near "Death Crossing". I loved their chicken fried steak and cream gravy, homemade yeast rolls with butter and honey, and their coconut cream pie! Another was Underwood's BBQ, out on East Division right next door to Candlelite Inn. Underwood's had a cafeteria style food line where you ordered the dishes you wanted, and then a sit-down area for eating. I remember the brisket and the banana pudding being especially tasty. The Candlelite Inn was good Italian food and always had a varied menu but we didn't go there a lot as we'd venture east to Fort Worth and go to The Italian Inn on East Lancaster. Now that was good Italian, at least as far as we knew. There you walked down from street level to enter and once inside there were booths with swinging privacy doors. It was a popular date spot later. Inside the booths the walls were covered with carved hearts and names. I loved the lasagna and bread pudding for dessert!

If we wanted Chinese or Asian food, there were simply no choices in Arlington back then. But that was OK because we had Jimmie Dip's on South University in Fort Worth near TCU. Back then Jimmie himself would greet and check on the customers. It was awesome, as you could order egg rolls, hot and sour soup, potstickers, and lo mein!

If we were wanting fried catfish, the most bang for the buck was Howard Johnson's, out on the newly completed DFW Turnpike. On Wednesday evenings they offered an all you could eat fried catfish dinner for $0.99. It was a bargain and it was good! A bunch of us guys would go there and attempt to break the bank. With the family we'd go to Bill Martin's Zuider Zee seafood restaurant on East Lancaster in Fort Worth. Everything was good but the hush puppies, fried clams and the key lime pie, were to die for.

Some of the other old Arlington restaurants were : Main Street Cafe; The Flying Dutchman; Shep's Fried Chicken; McIntosh; Youngblood's; Cattleman's; and a few more. But by the end of the '60s all sorts of restaurants came to town.

Thanks for all the great meals!
Danny

My First Car

1949 Ford Custom DeLuxe 2-Door Sedan
Arlington, Texas 1960

In 1960 we were still living in our home on University Drive near Arlington State College. At that time our family had only one car but was seriously considering a second. Dad had heard that Dr. Marcus, an old friend of Dad's from working at the college, had a used car for sale that might serve the family's needs. He lived on Barnes Drive relatively close to our house, just a mile or two away. Dad asked me I wanted to go with him the coming Saturday afternoon to take a look at it. For sure I wanted to go!! Dad didn't know too much about it, was it a 6 or a V8 engine? Was a two-door or four-door? What color was it? Was it an overdrive transmission? His answer was that we would find that out on Saturday. End of questions!

It seemed that time stood still until the designated time came. When we arrived the Ford was in the driveway. It was a black, V8, 3-speed manual, two sedan. Perfect!! I could visualize cruising through PALs or even venturing to The Bull Pen on East Abram, with dual exhausts flaming. I was on cloud nine. OK, back to earth, Dad bought the car for $375.00. I was ecstatic!! When we got her home Mom thought she was fine! Success! I secretly named her " Black Thunder". Don't ask, it seemed right at the time.

The first year we had her I couldn't drive (legally), but I washed her, vacuumed her, changed her fluids, etc. Dad had begun to hand me the tools when I was about 12, as we literally switched places and he became my helper. He would patiently provide instruction when needed, and stronger support when he felt it was appropriate. We changed the oil, gapped the plugs, adjusted the clutch, and rebuilt the brakes. (Just FYI, my Dad grew up without a father figure in Houston. He was hell-bent on giving his kids what he didn't have, a great Dad!! Those of you that knew Billy, know what I mean.) He would let me drive her on occasion, around the block or sometimes out in the country. The next year I was legal!! I scraped together $150.00, gave it to my Dad, and she was mine! I envisioned her as a hot rod but In reality, the poor little stock 239 cubic inch "flattie" was quite weak. It was rated at 100 horsepower, and maybe, had most of them on a good day.

Relatively soon after I started driving "Thunder", the clutch started failing. As an aside, "Thunder" had about 80,000 miles on her before we got her. Enough miles to loosen up the "three on the tree" shift linkage which made it perfect for "power shifting". For those not familiar with that term, it means shifting gears without ever lifting off the floored accelerator pedal. As a side note, that practice is very hard on the clutch! Anyway, I bought a heavy-duty pressure plate, a new clutch disc, and a new throw-out bearing, down at Walter's Auto on East Main. Got all the parts for about $36.00. A few hours of labor and she was good to go. Stabbing the 80-pound transmission in place, while lying on my back, was the most difficult, as it was a very precise operation. However, after the third time, I became very proficient. Somehow the failures of the transmission became more prevalent as the engine modifications yielded more power. Ha, imagine that! In similar fashion, I got very efficient at pulling out her engine. Each time the engine came out, changes were made, and it went back in with a little more power. It was in that timeframe that I had asked Don Wilson to help me acquire the parts necessary to build a streetable, stock-appearing, strong-running 276 cubic inch engine for "Thunder". Don and his brother Leon campaigned a Championship Flathead dragster that was one of the best. He helped me get the right parts. Like the "Little Deuce Coupe", she was balanced, bored, stroked, ported, and relieved, with an Isky 400 junior racing cam with stronger springs and adjustable lifters. She also got headers with dual exhausts, a modified intake manifold, shaved heads, a hotter distributor, and a bigger carb. She looked stock as a rock but had about 50% more horsepower. In her class, she was a street racer's ideal. We won our share! I even kept a tally book in the glovebox. I had one girlfriend who actually "loved" the lope of the cam and the way it literally "rocked" the entire car at idle! We fooled a lot of guys and had a lot of fun! One night we ran into a guy at PAL's who had just received (don't think had actually bought, it had to be a gift) a brand new, black Corvair Monza Spyder. The Spyders had special carburetion, a four-speed, and a turbocharger. He thought it ran well and wanted to try on "Thunder" for size. At that time 303 was a new blacktop south of town and ran from South Collins all the way to Rosedale in East Fort Worth. It had very little traffic and was the perfect place to test cars. Note: we did not race them but simply tested them against one another! Usually, we tested them two or three times if it was close. In this case, it wasn't, taillights were all he saw. In defense of the Corvair owner, the car was new to him and he wasn't used to the quirks of a turbo engine; however, I gave him several chances. Success! We won and didn't break anything!

"Thunder" and I had a great relationship. I would work and save money in order to lavish her with gifts, such as a new pair of Bucrons (street legal racing tires), a set of Smittys (free-flow mufflers), and a high-efficiency air filter. She would reciprocate by working her little heart out for me when it was time to run. Sadly, I did expose her to some unforgivable abuse on Halloween night in 1961. A few buddies and I were cruising a neighborhood off West Park Row just before Pantego Hill. We knew several girls who lived in that neighborhood and thought we might see them since it was Halloween. Sure enough, a group of them were walking between houses. We cruised past and waved, they waved back. We went down a ways and turned around. Little did the girls know, but we were loaded with water balloons. This was gonna be fun. We eased up on them and just as we were ready to let go, they hammered us with raw eggs! Some hit the target and even came inside through the window! We got away as fast as possible and quickly began to clean off the egg residue. Not a good night! That night we lost!

"Black Thunder" was a learning experience for me and tons of fun. What a ride!

Thanks for the memories Thunder,
Danny

31

PAL's, Arlington, Texas

Circa 1962

What an incredible place! We local teens desperately needed it at that time. Thank you, Mr. Lane! The name stood for Patricia Ann Lane, Mr. Lane's beautiful blonde daughter, AHS class of 1965. PAL's was literally Mel's Diner in American Graffiti, save the inside dining, and was just west of South Fielder on West Park Row in west Arlington. There were two rows of spaces, parallel to Park Row, separated by a long drive-way. The long driveway was designed to be an exit for both rows of cars but served as a literal parade runway for cars. We certainly had hot cars, cool cats, and plenty of awesome girls.

Fort Worth had The Clover and Dallas had Sivil's, but we had PAL's! Some kids had cars that had special "uniquely personalized" names back then, typically displayed on the back quarter panel or the trunk. Locally we had: Runnin' Bare, Great Balls of Fire, Rapid Rabbit, Draggin' Wagon, Flattop, White Lightnin', Cathy's Clown, Casper, Flathead Fever, Gray Goose, Runaway, and Teen Angel. In addition, some other popular names of the era were: Dreaming, Mr.Blue, Li'l Ol' Lady, Pancho Pride, Ace of Spades, Li'l Deuce Coupe, White

Lightnin', Black Widow, Lady Luck, Rambling Man, Thunder Road, One Eyed Jack, Gone Fishin', and Farmer's Daughter. Great names and great memories!

I digress, we could get a cherry Coke, an order of fries and a PAL's burger all for about 45 cents! What a deal! And as a bonus, we got plastic monkeys that had curvy tails that linked together, which could hang one from another, which could hang from one another, all hanging from the rearview mirror. Many kids had monkeys hanging a few feet long. Many of us would hot-foot it to the high school parking lot, jump in the car, and "speed-shift" to PAL's for lunch. Kids would gather every evening there for a "Coke date" or other constructive activities.

The cars would slowly "roll" through the drive-in runway touting their engine sounds and seducing potential drag racing opponents. Many of the cars had a modified exhaust system and a racing camshaft, yielding a beautiful-sounding "low rumble". Literally an engaging dance of power!

I've been told that some young car aficionados even attempted to use this venue to engage others in illegal street drag racing activities. Personally, I'm not certain of these allegations. However, I seem to recall having a "let's race" handheld sign, easily seen by the invited participant, available for use when the opportunity presented itself. I must say that I had many memorable, fun, and exciting times at this fine establishment!!

We were so fortunate to have had PAL's! Thank you, Mr. Lane!

Yours Truly,
Danny

32

Ridin' the Rails in 1962

Arlington, Texas

It was the fall of 1962. My buds and I could all drive. As a matter of course, we were always looking for fun and interesting things to do, in the pursuit of science, especially in the cover of darkness. Not sure where, but I had read about regular-sized cars of the 1950s being able to actually drive on railroad tracks. I have no idea where that came from! At any rate, the dimension between the center of the wheels on cars prior to 1958 was approximately the same as the dimension between the centerline of the railroad tracks. Wow, that was incredible! How smooth could that be? According to a reliable source, deflating the pressure of the front tires allowed them to sort or "contour around" the rails better, hence the driver was required to let go of the steering wheel and "have faith" that the car would track itself. Whew, sounds good on paper, but in real life, I wasn't sure! The problem is that if the car "derailed" it would be literally stuck there. There would be no escaping this predicament. And in the case of a "live track" a derailed confrontation with a locomotive would not end well. We'd actually have to engage a wrecker with a winch, to lift the car off the tracks. No way could we escape the wrath of many including our parents. As good as John D. was at getting us off the hook, even he couldn't win this one. He was good, but not that good! We had no girlfriends with us, this was way too dangerous and secure an operation to risk security containment.

Ok, so we decided that it would be, in the interest of science, a good idea to pursue this question of National Security and personal interest. My close friends, Johnny, Randy, Stewart, Gary, Dickie, Karl, and John were as adamantly committed to this stunning important experiment as I was. This could modify personal transportation options, as we knew it, for the future! So. We felt obligated to put this monumental challenge to the test. We had no one to question and/or confide in to help us with this predicament, or to advise us, but we moved forward.

The next week, we picked a time. Wednesday evening, next week. We had painstakingly measured the dimensions and felt confident of the potential results. We selected a place: the Great Southwest Industrial District. It had plenty of street crossings with roads that allowed for access and egress of the commercial tracks via cars. In addition, we could see and hear any train activity in the immediate area.

It was time: we had Dickie's '54 Chevy, Randy's '50 Olds, and my '49 Ford. We eased the cars onto the rails. We knew where we would exit and we knew the next road crossing where we could exit the rails. We eased some of the pressure out of the front tires. Dickie was first. He eased out onto the rails and rolled out onto the tracks. Success! He moved out toward the nearest track/road intersection and eased off the rails onto to roadway. It proved out!! Randy went next, then me, all successful! It was smooth beyond our expectations! We all enjoyed these activities on multiple occasions. It was fun! We never had an issue. We swore secrecy and told no one.

However, one day Dickie wanted to take this experiment to the next level. There was a rail crossing at South Bowen Road in west Arlington as well as a crossing at Handley Drive in far east Fort Worth. There was about four miles between the two. Johnny, me and John D. rode with Dickie, the rest of us drove to Handley where the crossing was. As a safeguard, we knew we could jump from the car if need be, so no huge risk, other than Dickie's car! He made the run! Awesome! After that, we decided to not press our luck any further with "Ridin' the Rails"! What a day!

Dickie was our hero that day!

Thanks Dickie!
Danny

33

The Music Talent

*The music talent at AHS in 1963, was unparalleled
at the high school level in Texas!*

We were so lucky to have a "top shelf" choir director in Jane Ellis, as well as a renowned band director in Dean Corey. Those two groomed our choir, The Choraliers, and Colt Band into top caliber performers. It was an absolute joy to be a spectator to their incredible and creative performances. Now, to be perfectly honest, I was not an appropriate candidate for either; however, that did not restrain me from appreciating both endeavors. Literally all of the participants In both groups were friends of mine. It was a big school but those of us who had been there for the duration knew most of our classmates. Miss Ellis actually wrote the AHS Fight song! And Dean Corey conducted such memorable renditions such as the famous "Peter Gunn" at a most memorable pep rally in 1962!! It literally stirred the student body! What an experience! The place was rocking! I'm so glad I didn't skip that one!

I want to acknowledge these two programs and the two leaders as being instrumental (you like that, Sheila?), in our music appreciation and overall academic growth! (Mom would be proud of that statement!). I did my best to guide and assist any of the female members of these groups that would accept my help, but, sadly, most weren't car girls! I tried, for their sake! You can lead a horse to water, but you can't make it drink!

We may not have won the game, but by golly we won the halftime! And, at graduation (yes I did graduate with a little Divine intervention, I might add) the choir's rendition of "You'll Never Walk Alone" was memorable to this day.

Thank you Miss Ellis and Dean Corey for such memorable times!

Danny

34

Rolling Hills Country Club

1954–2021. RIP, Place of Sweet Memories!

In about 1954 a few forward thinking families in Arlington joined forces to form what was to become Rolling Hills Country Club. They wanted a place to congregate, swim and play golf and tennis. W.O. Workman. Jack Harris, Dr. John Murchison, Les Eatson, Fran Miller and a handful of others comprised the small group. The initial name of the club was "WoHeLo", which were the first two letters of the words "Work, Health and Love". The land selected was a tract of 100 acres of dairy farmland, comprised of rolling hills and large oak trees and was located a mile or so west and about three miles north, of then, downtown Arlington. It cost the Charter Members an initial, partial payment of $50.00 for their membership. The initial projects included a small pool with a clubhouse as well as a nine hole golf course, both completed by 1956.

"WeHeLo" was a gathering place that was warm and friendly. With the opening of large companies like GM, and as the small town began to grow, so did "WeHeLo". The kids swam and had lots of parties. There were parties for teen dances, birthdays, and in addition, the adults celebrated anniversaries, and even memorial celebrations for departed friends. Many of the families bonded creating lifelong friendships.

In 1962 the club took big steps with a name change to "Rolling Hills Country Club", as well as the completion of their full 18 hole course. In the late '50s, a team of young girls and their moms set upon the task of hosting "dance" parties with their daughters. The first I recall was in '59 and most of us were 14. Our hostesses that evening were: Cathy Bontley, Jacque Deering, Margaret Floyd, Gretchen Weiker, Joyce Heffington, Carolyn Tinker, Suzanne Hightower, Barbara Meisner, Maudie Davis, Nancy Dickerson, and Jane Meier. The parties were very formal as the girls were all dressed up in beautiful, pastel formal dresses, the moms were as well! The dads usually were not there as they had bigger fish to fry! The boys were expected to wear nice sport coats with slacks or suits, both with ties. There was usually a band/combo, comprised of musically talented classmates including: Floyd Wine, Rusty Fowler, Jim Bergin, Ray Womack, Walter Taylor, Dan Rogers and a few others. There were even little dance cards with dance numbers and a blank line for the signature of the promised dance partner (it was kind of like a dance contract). One of the dances was deemed a "Sadie Hawkins" dance, which meant the girl asks the boy.

Side note: some of the moms looked so cute I attempted to alter the rules so that one dance could be a "Moms' rule dance", but I was unsuccessful. I did, however, manage to slip the system and get my "moms" dance during the evening. You should have seen her face when I held out my hand for hers. The "sweetest" dance of the night! No way, no reveal!

Now the rules were that if the boy, or girl, asked the potential dance partner for that designated dance, he/she had to accept that partner if not previously committed. As directed, only one dance was committed at a time, under the direction from the Dance Czar of the evening. The Dance Czar would also indicate which dance was next on the program. Another rule was that partners could not be duplicated, eliminating one dude hogging a particular girl. It actually worked pretty well and I applaud the creator of such a concept! At any rate it seems there were one or two of these dances a year and the everyone there had a good time. As was customary, the guest guys would attempt to dance with each of the hostesses. Hey, no problem for this guy, I was all over that challenge! Thanks to all the hostesses and moms for making it happen!

There were also lots of other parties but the dances stick out in my mind and that first one was very memorable. Our AHS class was fortunate enough to have our 25th and 50th reunions at Rolling Hills. Great times!

In 2021 the property was sold. Thanks for all the memories, old friend, may you R.I.P. knowing you fulfilled an important need for many!

Great times had by all,
Danny

╭────────────╮
│   **35**   │
╰────────────╯

The Best Snow Day of All!!

It was the fifth of January, a Friday, in 1962. We were juniors at AHS. It would have been a normal school day, however, as Harold Taft, channel 5 Chief Meteorologist had predicted the night before, there was a strong ice storm moving in from Wichita Falls overnight. It really happened. The school was called off. Darn! Ok, then, let's make the best of it I thought. A quick call to Gary Jinks got the ball rolling!

At that time Gary had a little 1960 green Volvo, a two-door sedan. It happened to have a trailer hitch with a small ball on it. It was serendipitous! A perfect appendage for a tow rope! I happened to have a ski rope and an inner tube. We were in business! Gary picked up Dickie Hirsch and John Donaghy up on his way to my house. Johnny Blesi had come over to my house before Gary arrived. The streets were perfect! A significant layer of snow is on top of a substantial layer of ice. There was absolutely no traffic on the streets. Varsity Circle just happened to be the optimum venue for the activity we had In mind: snow-tubing!!

First up was Dickie. We took off going south (clockwise) around the circle. The little Volvo performed well in those conditions, but not so much for the inner tube. You could kind of control the direction of the inner tube by shifting your weight from side to side. Although our butts were against the snow, the inner tube protected us as we slammed into the curbs. We took off. Dickie swerved from left to right then left as he hopped the curb and was thrown off in Brad Wileman's yard! We all roared with laughter as he rolled up like a donut in Brad's yard.

Next up was Blesi. The next stretch was fairly straight so he went a 100 yards or so, swerving between the curbs until we got near Jack Merbler's house. Then the centrifugal force landed him in the yard across from Jack. Donaghy was next and he landed up in Tommy Snider's yard. Gary was next as I got to drive. He made it several hundred yards to Beverly Stanford's driveway. I was last for the day and ended up in Dr. Wallace's yard. After a couple more turns around the circle, we were tired and traffic was beginning to get in the way. We called it a successful adventure. A great outing and no one got hurt!

My mom fixed us lunch and we were almost done for the day. Key word being almost.

We decided it might be fun to engage some girls in a snowball fight. Where should we go? We figured a few of them might be gathered near Duckett's house. We were right. There was Sylvia, Linda, Diane, Jan, Keith, Barbara, Lauren, Valerie and Janice. They were all kind of gathered on Linda's front porch. These girls must have gotten a telegraph we were coming for them, as the were loaded for bear. As we got closer we could almost smell the pending danger. We were outnumbered and outgunned! Each girl carried a medium-sized canvas bag. My gosh, they were ammo bags! They had an arsenal of dye-infused, semi-frozen, water balloons. Holy smokes! We were slammed like Custer at Little Big Horn!! We turned tails and got the heck out of there!

All in all, the best snow day ever!
Thanks for the fun,
Danny

36

Arlington Teachers

In Arlington, we were blessed to have an abundance of wonderful, caring, and talented teachers. Arlington, post WWII, was a growing community, morphing from a little rural burg to a pulsating, modern college town. As such, our schools multiplied and along with that growth came the demand for exceptional teachers, administrators and coaches, who were some of both. We were fortunate to have leaders like Woodrow Counts and James Martin, as insightful superintendents and an army of dedicated principals and school board members to lead and guide the Arlington Independent School District forward.

It's almost impossible to quantify the number and dedication of our teachers/coaches in the post-war years of the growth of the Arlington Independent School District. Us kids of that time were, indeed, the benefactors of such growth and synergy. It began just before or right after WWII with the hiring of Dean Corey and Jane Ellis, talents extraordinaire, as far as band and choir were concerned. Then they hired Mayfield Workman, an up-and-coming young football head coach. By 1950 Arlington had a solid base to build upon! Then came Miss Amos, an English leader, Mrs. Pope, a chemistry phenomenon, as well as Mrs. Clements, for biology and chemistry, Mrs.

Baker for math, and Paul Booher for shop and industrial arts and the Butler sisters for history and math. Shortly thereafter, Mr. Wood, Mr. Dunn, Mr. Miller, Mr. Stanford, and Mr. Bebensee came on board, all as principals and administrators. Now, Arlington had the building blocks in place needed for a growing, pulsating community. Mr. Webb and Mr. Curlee were soon thereafter. All told, the AISD leaders were at the top of their game when it came to the hiring of excellent professionals. Soon thereafter, Mayfield hired Doyle Malone, O'Neil Harris, Guy Shaw Thompson, Elo Nohavitza, Harold Hill and Weldon Wright as his assistants. Now, folks, that was a team!!

Our team of teachers and coaches was likely the best in Texas, for a community our size, thanks to our leaders!!

So, I can only relate to my particular teachers, but I was lucky enough to have a first-class group! For the first grade at West Side, I had Mrs. Brem. She was very nice and I liked her a lot. Second grade was Mrs. Wolverton (Ann's mom) and she was very forgiving (as needed). Third grade was Miss Stewart. Ok, I was in love! She was young (only 13 years older), absolutely beautiful and very perky!! I actually loved her!! Anyway, she got married toward the end of the year and SHATTERED my childhood dreams! We could have been soooo happy in Tahiti!! Fourth grade brought Mrs. Arthur, a great teacher and a friend of my mom. Fifth grade was Mrs. Stanford, a neighbor and friend of my parents. Very good teacher and I liked her daughter, Beverly. No luck there!! Sixth brought Mrs. Wommack, Ray's mom. We had a kid in her class, Billy Lassen, who could multiply a three-digit number by another three-digit number, in his head and never write anything down but the answer on the blackboard!! Even Joyce couldn't keep up with that!! Seventh brought Miss Bayless. I had no clout with her, but her nephew, Ikey, was a nice guy!

On to Ousley. I loved Mrs. Hughes, Miss Goodman (1959 white/red Olds, 88 Hardtop), Mrs. Roark and of course the coaches, O'Neil Harris, Doyle Malone, Harold Hill, and Weldon Wright, our coaches, all at Ousley.

Then AHS, with Mrs. Mikusek, Mrs. Holder, Mrs. Curry, Edgar Cullers, and always, Miss Ellis. Those are my favorites, whom are yours?

Thanks,
Danny

37

Our Coaches

It's difficult to place the "value of influence" a caring, yet forceful, Coach (yes, I choose to capitalize the word much like Dad or Mom) has on the person electing to receive that instruction! This is a "Coach" appreciation story.

Arlington was really growing after WWII. We were a college town with a thriving sports program, at all levels, excelling in football, thanks to Coach Gilstrap and Coach Tinker at the junior college level, and filtering down. Our community was absolutely blessed to have been able to attract an incredible array of high-powered, dynamic young coaches for our junior high and high school programs. The AISD leaders, Coach Mayfield Workman and the Arlington political powers, including young Tommy Vandergriff, enticed an array of talent to be a part of the Arlington program. By the mid-fifties they had attracted Doyle Malone, Guy Shaw Thompson, Sam Curlee and O'Neil Harris. A couple years later they added Harold Hill, Elo Nohavitza and Weldon Wright. Now, arguably, with that team of excellent coaches, Arlington was poised to rival any district in the state of Texas!

What is a coach? To me "Coach" is a reveered title that very few people have. It's kind of a blend of teacher, caretaker, influencer, physical trainer, mentor, drill sargent and admired friend. It's an individual who's attempting to teach you something that he/she had already done at a very high level, and excelled at. The title is earned and sticks, forever. All my coaches were still "Coach", well after they were trying to coach me, even after they had retired from coaching. It's a lifetime title bestowed upon few educators. I'm not aware of anyone, outside immediate family, that can so profoundly influence an individual. At 100 kids per year for a full career of coaching, that "Coach" influences about 3000 young people. What a responsibility! In Arlington we were truly blessed with great "Coaches"! I am thankful to have had so many!

Thanks "Coach",
Danny

38

A Dog Named Flash!

It was 1961 in Arlington, Texas. My buds and I could all drive and were having a grand time fooling around with cars. We'd gather at PAL's or the A&P parking lot across the street, on nights we could convince our folks we had to go study at a friend's house or the library. That "line" worked some of the time!

One evening, huddled around the parking lot visiting with other like minded, studious youths, we learned of a dog that resided down on South Davis, that liked to race cars. Of course, our cars weren't hot rods at that time, but we figured we could beat a dog! John D., Gary J., Don S. and Dickie H. all piled into my old Ford and went on a hunt for the dog. We knew he was on South Davis at a cross street, and that his yard was fenced. After a few trips between Southwood and Tucker we found him at the southwest corner of Marshalldale. None of us knew who lived there but we knew kids nearby. The yard was chain link fenced and was fairly deep along South Davis. It was about 70' of runway for the dog.

He was a medium sized, German Shepherd mix, brown and black, and fairly young. I stopped the car and several of us got out to check him out. The name on his collar was "Flash".

He loved barking and running up and down that fence line. We didn't want to create a commotion, so we bid him farewell, hopped in the Ford and began to leave going south toward 303. "Flash" instinctively lined up with the front of the car, almost on point, and waited, anticipating our departure. As soon as the car moved he took off like a rocket to the end of his fence! Wow! We were all impressed.

We came back many times in many different cars and seriously tried to outrun him. We never could beat Flash! What an animal!

RIP Flash,
Danny

39

Flo (A.K.A. Black Thunder)

The tale of Flo, later named Black Thunder,
a black 1949 Ford, 2-door Custom, from Arlington, Texas.
Told from her point of view.

It was March of 1949. My future family, the Marquises were seated in the office of Jerry Mebus, a partner in the Bob Cooke Ford dealership, on East Division in Arlington, Texas. Dr. Marquis was a professor of English at ASC, and was there with his lovely wife Elizabeth and their two young daughters Mary, who was eight and Meredith, who was ten. Cars were still in short supply so they were placing an order for ME, a 1949, Black, two door Custom. Together, they ordered me with a V/8, an optional radio and an optional heater. Elizabeth liked the stainless steel beauty rings and Dr. Marquis agreed. Mr. Mebus filled out the order sheet, took a deposit check and thanked the family for the business. I was to be built in Dallas and was scheduled to arrive on or about the 20th of April.

The day I arrived, the service guys cleaned me all up and Mr. Mebus called the family. I was sparkling from bumper to bumper and looked quite spiffy with my new black paint shining, with beauty rings and grey interior. When they arrived the girls squealed with joy and the parents smiled as I was just right for their nice young family. They named me Flo, after an aunt they all loved, but had recently passed. They drove me to their home on Barnes Drive, just west of South Davis in Arlington. What a nice and calm home for me to enjoy. As the girls got older Dr. Marquis taught them to drive me, even with the standard transmission and three on the tree. All of the family treated me kind and never abused me. Only once was Meredith a little rough on the clutch as she couldn't get the hang of "easing out" when starting off from a stoplight. I served them well for nine years.

Then the inevitable happened! I was getting older and newer, younger models were more attractive with beautiful color schemes, beautiful body lines, and amenities like automatic transmissions and air conditioning. My first family sold me like an inanimate object. Bummer! Looking back though, it was a very nice but dull existence. I never got to go over 60 MPH, never had any thrilling close calls, and never had any fun or excitement.

Now Dr. Marquis had worked with Billy Armstrong at ASC and somehow Billy found out Dr. Marquis was selling the Ford. Billy came over to look me over one Saturday morning with his 13-year old, red-headed son, Danny. Billy was looking me over thoroughly, and Danny, meanwhile, wanted to look under my hood and fondle my shifter. But hey, all ended well and I had a new home! The Armstrong family lived on University Drive and I was to be their first, second car. They were a nice family with two brothers, Danny and Johnny, and a younger sister, Jan. Billy's pretty wife was named June and she drove me a lot. The younger kids paid me little mind but Danny was very attentive. He'd wash me and wax me and clean my engine and interior. When he and I were alone he'd always either sing to me or talk to me. He called me "baby sister" when we were alone and "Thunder" when others were around. Once he even painted my lug nuts pink like a girl's toenails! On occasion, while washing me, he would stick the water hose up my tailpipe and let the water run up into my muffler. It was like an enema! It was as if he wanted to rust out the innards of my muffler, which would make me very loud. Why on earth would he do that? When he did I felt somewhat violated! Over time I got over it, and eventually learned to enjoy it, in a cleansing sort of way.

As Danny got a little older Billy began to let him drive me. First just around the block then longer ventures. By the time Danny took his driving test he was a fairly accomplished young driver, thanks to me. When Danny got to high school he literally took me over as his car, "Black Thunder", (my new name). Now this kid and I had some fun and many adventures together, I assure you. On our first ride alone together, he decided it was time to see how fast I could go. My speedometer only went to 100 but I'd never gone more than 65 until that night. We picked up a couple of his buds, Gary Jinks and Dickie Hirsch, at PAL's and headed out to a partially finished section of what was going to be 303 in south Arlington. It was jet black but my little headlights were aglow with anticipation. There were no other lights so we had to be able to stop before we ran out of road. I was pretty sure my brakes would save us, if need be. We got on the fresh pavement and began to roll. I responded to Danny's right foot and we rolled up through the gears, going into third at about 50. A long way to go, I thought, to peg my speedo! We hit 60, then 70, then 80, then 90, and it was over! Barricades ahead! My brakes kept us safe that night. I really don't think I could have gone any faster that night even if the road went on forever. We obviously needed more power!

It wasn't long before Danny got enough money to rebuild my engine (with a few extra performance parts included). I also got a stronger clutch, dual exhaust with Smittys, and better tires. Now, we were ready to hit the road again, just us two this time. We drove to a secluded place of the highway and turned the horses loose! Wow, I felt as if my power had doubled! We hard-pegged my speedo with a little to spare! That began a new chapter. Lots of fun times were had. I felt as if I were finally really living! When we happened to be in a situation where we wanted to scientifically test my newfound performance, as we pulled beside our test partner, Danny would always say to me "ok, little sister, let's show them your taillights", and we usually did!

There were a few girls along the way but most weren't automotive enthusiasts and couldn't appreciate my hidden beauty. One, however, did and I really liked her. My new camshaft yielded quite a "lope" at idle and I rocked a little as a result. She loved that! I felt appreciated.

I had a great and exciting life with Danny and enjoyed almost every day. He did get us into trouble a couple of times but we made it through. One Halloween night we got egged by a bunch of rowdy girls! Another time we got airborne on Hiccup Hill and another time a blowout going a little fast on West Division. It was a sad day for me when he sold me to return to a dull and unappreciated lifestyle. I guess you could say a normal life for an older, "little sister". But maybe, someday, we'll meet again. I sure hope so!

All my best,
Little Sister

40

A Day at Lucas Park

Arlington, Texas
Circa 1962

Lucas Park was a haven for teenagers in the '50s and '60s. The property was located at the northeast corner of California Lane and South Bowen Road in far southwest Arlington. It was about 50 acres, covered with large oak trees, and included a swimming pool with an adjacent recreation and picnic area, a rental go-cart track, and a private airport. Kids would frequent there for miles around to swim, picnic, ride go-carts, and enjoy a summer day. Older kids and adults would take private flying lessons and would frequent the skies with touch-and-go landings. There were many grassy areas between the trees warmly inviting sunbathers with their towels. In the hot summer sun, there was lots of lovingly applied Coppertone or Baby Oil in the pool area. A lot of AHS social events and birthday parties took place at this venue as it was so much more private and controlled than the municipal facilities.

The Lucas family home was on the property. Young Donny Lucas was envied by many of us younger guys. He had total access to the entire park, private privileges with aircraft, and he drove a nice 1957 Blue Chevy BelAir Hardtop! It was a two-four, 270 HP 283 with a three-speed overdrive tranny. Don't some guys get all the breaks?

Oh well, some folks had to get back to work, applying Coppertone to those "hard to reach" places! I thought to myself as Donny drove off "Haha, Donny, who's lucky now"?

It was a great class outing in 1962. Tons of fun at an incredible and unique venue.

Thanks Donny,
Danny

41

Fun Times

Roller Coaster Hill/Hiccup Hill/Feather Beach!
Circa 1962

During the early '60s, in Arlington, Texas, there were three places that were known to almost all high school kids. After a movie or a burger and cherry coke at PAL's, there was substantial traffic headed west toward Lake Arlington. First destination was "Roller Coaster Hill". Turning south off Arkansas Road onto Perkins Road, along the east side of Lake Arlington were a series of fairly intense, rolling hills in a row. At 40 MPH, they were barely a thrill. BUT, at 60 or above they became very interesting: hence, the name, "Roller Coaster Hill"! Many nights of fun were had going down Perkins Road! The "Saving Grace", was the times we were most adventurous with our driving experiences paralleled the times when we had the slowest cars. Otherwise, we may have gotten into deep trouble! Also, another consideration was, at that time the southeast side of the lake was still mostly rural and undeveloped so there was very little traffic, especially at night.

Going south, Perkins Road ended at Pleasant Ridge Road. Turning right led to Feather Beach, which we'll get back to in a minute, but turning left on Pleasant Ridge led back toward Bowen Road in Dalworthington Gardens, a small community southwest of Arlington. From Perkins, as you headed east on Pleasant Ridge toward "Hiccup" you'd go through an S curve a short distance past Little Road and then the road was a straight shot eastward for about three miles. The first mile or so the road was slightly uphill and the last mile and a half the road was downhill and then it flattened out. So, right in the middle lay "Hiccup Hill"! It was a rather pointed hill not rounded over like most. As I recall, addressing the hill from the west netted the best result. If the wind was blowing just right and the car was not too overloaded, a full throttle right out of the final S turn could yield a speed of about 75 by the time the hill was crested. As we crested the car seemed as if it was airborne for a second or so and we all bumped our heads on the roof! Sometimes the roofs got dented! It's my understanding that a few cars ended up in the ditch on the downside touchdown! Fun times!

Now, if you turned right at the previous intersection, Pleasant Ridge Road dead-ended into Lake Arlington at Feather Beach. By day it was a small secluded beach with no homes in sight. There were a few picnic tables and some picnic cooking grills and very little traffic. But by night, that's another story. Several cars would be there with couples enjoying the sparkling stars as well as the sparkling eyes of their sweethearts. It was a "parking" rendezvous not a parking lot! Some were in love some were not. A few steamy windows, a few slammed doors. Many promises made, some kept, most broken! A special place, not soon to be forgotten!

Great times, great memories and a few dents!

Will remember those times forever,
Danny

42

Friends! (Pre-Adult)

I'm not sure, but I think almost everything possible has been said or written or sung about friends. So, this is a short story. We've all been blessed to have that special friend, our best friend, at that particular point in time, that above all others, is most tuned in to our needs. They were the ones that we could depend upon for our privacy, and that we needed most of all at that time for their support. I have had a few, mostly boys but some girls, and truly cherish that, I guess, love. Thank you!

The circles of friends continue to draw me into their intricacies. How they overlap integrate and blend with other circles of friends. The neighborhood circle, the sports circle, the scouts circle, the choir circle, the literary circle, the dance class circle, the car club circle, the political circle, and the family circle. It all never ceases to amaze me. I feel so fortunate to have been able to "overlap" our circles of friendships with so many of you. Just a thought, be thankful!

Best wishes, friends,
Danny

43

"B" Team Football

AHS 1961

In Arlington, in 1961, both Carter Junior High and Ousley Junior High, for the first time, joined forces to come together as the 1961 "B" Team AHS Colts! The previous year we competed against each other, but now we were "B" team brothers. Coach Guy Shaw Thompson was one of our coaches and the other was Coach Harold Hill, moving up to AHS with us from Ousley. These two coaches were charged by Coach Workman to blend these two teams into a cohesive, developmental team for the future. They were apparently successful as the young team yielded a fine record.

Carter brought a great number of really good ball players to the mix. Guys like Jimmy Murphy at quarterback, Danny Johnson at offensive tackle, Jimmy Houston at running back, David Bane at halfback, Alvin Hartz at defensive and offensive end, Jimmy Biggers at offensive and defensive end, David Love at halfback, Bill Hubbard at guard, John Chesnut at end, Lance Utterback at end, George Devault at cornerback, Blair Kitterman at defensive tackle, Billy Pierson at linebacker and many others. Many of these players were athletically gifted enough to play both ways.

In a like manner, Ousley had a lot of very good players they brought to mix as well. We had a backfield group of Rusty Workman, Nicky Joy, Joe Skelton, Dennis Carlson, Jimmy Falvo. We had Roger Fanning at quarterback, Stewart DeVore, Jack Merbler, Andy Chambers, Gary Harwell, and Tim Gillespie as linemen. We also had Gary Page, defensive secondary, and many others. We had many two-way players as well.

As an added bonus, we got a handful of excellent players just moving to Arlington from other towns. These guys were not just good players, they were impact players and we were lucky to get them. Brad Jessup came to us from out of state and was a running back. Mike Soward was a really fast receiver from Grand Prairie. And then, like icing on the cake, we got Leslie Mendenhall, a hard-hitting middle linebacker with a quarterback's intuition, from Arlington Heights in Fort Worth. These three wildcards were a great addition to our team and we were blessed to have them!

We were also fortunate to have Randy Larson and Jimmy Norwood as team managers. These two performed countless and thankless duties with zero complaints.

Our first few practices reflected that there was still a Carter versus Ousley mentality. Then, after a few days of practice, our scrimmages evolved to defense against offense, the way it should be. At that point in time, we became a team! Now, we were the AHS Colts and by golly we were feeling good about our chances to be a competitive team.

Our first four games were all close but we came out ahead in the end. We were feeling good. The next game we came up against Garland, in their house. Coach Hill and Coach Thompson had us as prepared as we could be but it was a tough, low-scoring game. They were our best opponents so far. The game ended tied, 14 all. Our next game was at home against the Grand Prairie Gophers. They were a solid team with great skill players. We were behind late in the fourth quarter by seven points, but we were driving at their 30. Coach called for a right side end around with Dennis as the designated ball carrier. Alvin was at right end and I was a left. (Alvin was a much better blocker than I was so it didn't bother me one bit that we were going right as I could watch it much easier that way.) Alvin took care of the defensive end and Rusty followed him to take out the linebacker. Nicky followed Rusty and wiped out the safety. Dennis scampered into the end zone without contact! Ten seconds left and we were one point behind. Coach Hill called for Rusty off our left tackle, Stewart. Between Stewart and Andy, Rusty bulldozed in for two points and we won! I think that was our best win of the season. Everyone was ecstatic! Still undefeated (so far)!

We won the next game against the Rebels of North Richland Hills thanks to the outstanding play of David, Mike H., Mike S., Billy, Danny J., Roger, Les, Joe, Jimmy H. and Jimmy B., Falvo, Gary H., Gary P., Tim, David L. and Jack.

Only one more game to go, the Wichita Falls Coyotes. They just so happened to have one of the best running backs in the state, Larry Shields. He was in the process of breaking Texas state rushing records held by his older brother Ronny. Lovely. Anyway, we throttled them down to 14 points in the first half thanks to our solid defense but they held us down to seven. It was about then that we came to the painfully apparent conclusion that we only had one player that was fast enough to run Shields down in the open field and only one strong enough to bring him to the ground. Sadly, those attributes belonged to two different players! He was killing us! Through the second half the weather began to cool down and we did as well due to some injuries of key players. Shields didn't cool off. He broke loose for a 99 yard run at the end of the game. We lost. We played a really good team a hard-fought game, we just couldn't find a way to win. It was a quiet, long bus ride back to Arlington.

At 8-1-1, it was a great season. Thankfully, I was lucky to be a part of it and to have made so many new friends and to maintain the old ones!

Love you guys!
Danny

44

Senior Year, 1963

(Kids: How I Met Your Mother)

It was the last semester of the last year of high school! I was fortunate enough to have Mr. Edgar Cullers as my mechanical drawing teacher. Now Mr. Cullers was not too enthusiastic or entertaining, as he was pretty much down to business. Precise dimensions, proper perspective, and printing excellence! Those were his criteria for a very good grade! I was a part of an awesome class of overachievers. Contrary to public belief, my classmates and I took this class very seriously. It required a great deal of concentration and dedication to put on paper what was an oblique dream or sketch in the mind or imagination of an inventor or aeronautic engineer or entrepreneurial inventor (not sure about you, but I am impressed). Mr. Cullers was a very nice teacher and would accommodate special student needs. Firsthand, I know he helped students with their special needs regarding schedule changes. He was a very caring teacher.

For me, this was the perfect class. I already knew the material (duh, my dad taught college-level mechanical drawing), I could print better than anyone I knew, and I was friends with the family. So, all and all, Mr. Cullers was one of my favorite teachers.

In those days we had student assistants to accumulate the attendance of each class each day. These dedicated young students would make their assigned rounds each day to retrieve the attendance data from the assigned classes. Now, of course, I couldn't allocate my time as I was far too busy taking care of other business, however, many other dedicated students did so, and I certainly appreciated such dedication.

In our particular class, we had a specifically assigned attendance collector. A few weeks into the semester I began to notice her. She was precisely on time each day. She was always nicely dressed and very friendly. She actually smiled at me on occasion! She was very pretty and she had a confident air about her. How could I not know her? I thought I knew everybody! Apparently not. Ok, I needed to find out more about this girl! Of course, the time allocation would have to be in between my studies and other pressing responsibilities, but this was an important task and I had to dedicate whatever efforts and time required to answer my own pressing questions!

I did! She was perfect! 61 years later she is still perfect and the love of my life! For all of the above reasons, Mr. Cullers is my most favorite teacher of all time.

Thank you, Mr. Cullers,
Danny

45

The "Hands Down" Best Pep Rally of All Time (For Us)!!

It was the fall of 1962. It was a Friday about 9:30 that morning. We had a big game ahead of us against the Grand Prairie Gophers. They were good! First on the agenda, we had Coach Elo Nohavitza give us a "rock 'em sock 'em" motivational speech, not unlike Coach Calhoun (Sid Caesar) in the movie Grease. Anyway, the program moved on to a couple of skits put on by the different classes. The cheerleaders and ball players put on the skits and all were entertaining. Roger F. and Ann W. were presented as Mr. and Miss AHS Spirit Representatives for 1963! All in all it was a really great pep rally, perhaps the best of the year, to date. Now, it was time for the band to send us into the next stratosphere of high school frenzy.

We had a fantastic band, commandeered by Dean Corey with a phenomenal array of talented musicians. The rendition of the moment was the theme from Peter Gunn. The band had played the theme previously, but never with the enthusiasm and precision of this day's performance. The band started the rendition and it was moving, to say the least. We were all feeling the intensity of the moment.

As much as we all were feeling the moment, none felt it as much as one classmate. All of a sudden, my friend Wesley Huckabay, jumped from the fifth row down to the gym floor and began to dance the twist! He was very good! The entire gym went crazy! We were all cheering Wesley on and he met the call. It was a great pep rally and one none of us will forget! Without doubt, the best pep rally of all time!

Thanks Wesley,
Danny

46

Early Jobs: Successes and Failures!

It indeed has been an interesting ride. My first real job was door to door selling of "Spudnuts"! "Spudnuts" came into being in Arlington in about 1956 and were simply donuts made with potato flour. I was eleven and in the fifth grade at West Side Elementary School, in Arlington, Texas. My good buddy, James Graham, already had a route with "Spudnuts" and encouraged me to join him. They had a bakery operation next to the 7/11 on Park Row, across from AHS. That's where they fried up the delicacies, and boxed them up for the route salesmen. The "Spudnuts" were actually very good! A little heavier than typical donuts, but still, they were very good! I loved them! Kind of like KrispyKremes today. Anyway, when I joined James, he had actually saved up $65.00 from his sales efforts with "Spudnuts"! At $1.20 per dozen, the sales representative made $0.20 per. $ 65.00 is a lot of 20-cent dozens!! James was very successful! James lived over on Hollis Street, near Saint Maria Gorretti. Anyway, James and I would meet up with our Regional Route Manager, Jimmy Jacobsen, and he would dole out our allocation of dozens of "Spudnuts". We had our bikes rigged out to carry up to 12 dozen. My career lasted about six weeks and I considered it a huge success.

Shortly thereafter, the company was closed, but hey, James and I made our big bucks! At 20 cents a dozen times 12 dozen, that was $2.40 for about an hour a day! As a bonus, Jimmy would bring us each a small bag of 6 "Spudnuts", a nice little snack while delivering the orders. "Spudnuts" was a great experience! Success!

About that timeframe, I had begun helping Dad with re-painting our house. He taught me to thoroughly clean and prepare the surface to be painted. He also taught me to apply enough paint to cover but not so much a to create runs, as well how to keep the paint off the areas not intended to be painted, and finally, to clean up properly. So, all in all, I did a pretty good job for a kid. I painted a couple houses for neighbors then came to a reality check. Yes, I could do this work. Yes, it's lonely working by yourself. Is it somewhat dangerous work with ladders and such? Could I get hurt? Maybe, like when I fell 6' into a rose bush! Anyway, summer was almost over and school would start soon, so surely, next summer would present brighter opportunities! It did! So the house painting was a good experience and a success in a sense that it showed me I could do it, but that I wanted to have a job that was more social and enjoyable.

Next up was a paper route. I worked for the Arlington Citizen Journal. My little route was from University Drive, north up South Davis to Abram, then east on Abram to Summit, than south to West Second, up and down West Second as well as West Fourth, Shady Lane, Varsity Circle and University Drive. It was a route of approximately 105 subscribers. It took me about an hour. I didn't appreciate the dogs that chased me. (Oh, what I would have given for a current taser)! My takeaway from this job was that without a scooter, forbidden by Mom, it was fruitless. A total failure on a bike! Loser!

Next up, I went to work at a Humble gas station on Park Row, just one block west of New York, owned by Dennis Diggins. I made 75 cents per hour. A great job! I got to "fill her up with ethyl" or pump "two dollars of regular"! "Check the oil and tires" were standard requests, and of course, washing the windshield! On rare occasions we'd get a customer with a high-performance model and I'd give that one special attention and attempt to visit with the owner. Most of those owners were more than happy to talk to a kid interested in their particular car. I especially remember my Little League coach, Jim Jones, as he was a regular customer. He had a special order, black 1959 Chevy El Camino with a three deuce 348, and a four speed with a positraction rear axle. Success!

The next summer I worked for Herb Turner, a super nice boss, at his lumber yard on the corner of South Davis and West Main. I got to learn about dimensional lumber, fasteners, doors, hardware and all the other items typically in a lumber yard. I'd work part of the week at the lumber yard, then part of the week with my buddy, Dickie Hirsch. Dickie had an agreement with a couple of home builders that were building homes in the newly developed Woodland West neighborhood near South Bowen and Norwood Lane. The agreement entailed setting the triangular, pre-fabricated trusses on top of the exterior wall framing, already in place. Once in place the trusses provided the structural framing for the roof and ceiling.

Now THIS was an exciting job! The trusses came to the job site on a large special built trailer and offloaded by a construction fork lift owned by the truss company. They were banded together in batches of about twelve. We had to break the bands and place the trusses in the correct order they were going to be placed. Everything we did was by hand as we had no access to the forklift. Our truss team was usually Dickie and me and one or two other guys we'd find. Once the trusses were placed in order, the team member on the ground would manhandle the truss to Dickie and me standing on the upper plate of the framed exterior walls. NOW, this was the tricky part. We had to lift the truss about chest high and walk it to the far end while balancing atop the exterior walls. Mind you these walls were 4" wide and about 8' in the air. Then we would nail it in place and brace it off. Next we walk back down to the other end on top of the wall and grab the next one. There would be about 40 trusses on a typical house. It made for a long day but it was very satisfying and we had fun doing it! As a team we made about $250.00 per house. Success!

There were a few other jobs but this story is already too long. All were great experiences and some were really fun.

Thanks to all the bosses,
Danny

47

Patty

We were fortunate enough to have a very active foreign student exchange program in Arlington, beginning in the early '60s. Our school system must have had leaders with extreme foresight and political influence to be approved to enter into such a limited program. Hats off to those folks! As best I can recall, that program started at AHS in about 1960. That year we sent one of our finest Colts, Bruce Malone, to Germany and we had gotten a student from Norway named Bjorn Lindvig. At that time we were sophomores and he was a senior. Very nice all-around guy, as best I could tell, but a little far-removed from lowerclassmen. The next year we were juniors and our classmate Brad Jessup went to The Philippines in the program. He lived in a thatch home, and he became thoroughly immersed in their culture. He wore a large straw hat and homemade sandals. He was one of them! His integration and literal immersion into that culture was totally successful. In our senior year we sent Gretchen Weiker to Holland and we got in return, Patty Contador-Soko from Santiago, Chile.

Patty arrived at Love Field in late August 1962 after a tiring, 4-day, multi-leg flight from Santiago, Chile. There was a welcoming committee to greet her and yours truly was lucky enough to be there. I even got to carry her luggage! As circumstance would have it, we happened upon Johnny Crawford, the teenage western TV star, at the arrival gate. Johnny played Mark McCain, Lucas's son on The Rifleman, a very popular show. He was very cordial, welcomed the girls' attention, and took several photos with them. Patty's host family were all there to greet her including Doctor Paul Bontley, his beautiful wife Zora, my friend and classmate Cathy and her younger sister, Beth. IMHO, they were the perfect host family for Patty.

Patty was a smart, outgoing, confident, warm, courteous and beautiful young lady. Her home was Santiago, Chile, the largest city in Chile, and she was from a successful family of three siblings. She went to good schools and was among the brightest in her class. She excelled at AHS as she was good at math, excellent in language arts, a Choralier, confident enough to participate in any activity, a very attentive listener, loved our music and dances, and generally a fun girl! She was involved with the Student Council, she was voted sweetheart of the Valentine Dance, She could speak and write better than most of us, she loved football, pep rallys and school dances. She devoured hamburgers and chocolate cake and she loved Zora's Thanksgiving dinner most of all. She loved American cars and going to PAL's where she enjoyed cherry Cokes with a plastic monkey hanging from the straw. She totally fit in to our culture and environment. Without a doubt, she was perfect for us and I think we were perfect for her. Patty was completely embraced by our class and fit into each and every situation.

A funny quirk was that for some unknown reason Patty didn't want to reveal her actual age. She made us all believe she was a year younger than we were. It was 53 years later that the truth was finally revealed. Funny!

All the US exchange students gathered for a two week exit tour before returning home. A highlight for Patty was a stop at Washington, D.C. where the kids met President Kennedy. Patty learned to appreciate and love our country and our people, just as we loved and appreciated her. When she got here she could not understand why we elected to call ourselves "Americans", while there were many other counties located in North and South America that didn't do so. When she left she said she totally understood!! We were THE Americans!

After Patty went back to Chile she kept in touch with her closest AHS friends. She actually attended our 30th year class reunion and was the "hit" of the activities! We were all so surprised and happy to see her. Although we weren't that close, she was caring enough to wish me well when I was recovering from surgery in 2019. What a nice and unexpected gesture of care and kindness. She was truly beautiful inside and out!

Unfortunately, Patty passed September 25, 2019, a sad day.
RIP my friend,
Danny

48

The Cars of Our Time

From 1954 to 1964, in Arlington, Texas!

Let me preface: this is kind of a "car guy" story, so some may not appreciate it. I don't apologize. What an awesome time for automotive evolution! We car guys were in heaven! All the manufacturers were stepping up their game in terms of performance! There were 'Vettes with 4-speed gearboxes, fuel injection and 315 hp and 4.56 rear axle gears. There were 413, 425 hp, Plymouth Cross Ram Belvederes. Olds had their J-2, tri-power option available. There were 390, 401 hp, Ford Starliners, there were 409, 4-'speed, Super Sport Chevys, and Super Duty Ventura, 3 deuce Pontiacs! Even Chrysler offered a cross ram 413 with two fours and a 4-speed in their 300G! By '57 Bonnevilles had mechanical fuel injection as well. Even Rambler had electronic fuel injection scheduled for the '57 Rebel but they ran into technical difficulties. Chrysler's high-performance products had electronic fuel injection available in '58, but it too was an unsuccessful venture. '57 Fords were available with superchargers and by the early '60s, turbochargers were available on some GM models. What a glorious time!

Back to reality in Arlington, Texas. We had some fabulous cars in Arlington! Since 1958 I had noticed a car I absolutely coveted. It was owned by Jerry Caddell. Jerry was a few years older and was the older brother of Beverly Caddell, a band majorette, she was one year older and was a beautiful and smart girl.

All that aside, Jerry's car was a bronze and cream, '51 Ford Victoria Hardtop, Draggin' Wagon". For power, Jerry had cannibalized a 1957 Corvette. Not just any Corvette, but one with a 270HP, 2 four, solid lifter engine and close ratio, 4-speed transmission and to top her off, '57 Caddy hubcaps. What a combo!! High-performance Corvette running gear in a '51 Victoria body! I thought it was the ultimate dream car! We had John Gumpert's "Rapid Rabbit", a 1958 Pontiac Catalina with a Super Duty 389, 3 deuces, a 4-speed automatic and a 4:11 rear end! Killer!! We had Jimmy D's '32, "Little Deuce Coupe". It had a 256 Mercury mill with Edelbrock aluminum heads, a 3 deuce manifold with 3 Strombergs, and an Isky racing cam, all hooked up to a Lincoln Zephyr tranny. My friend, Don Smith had a black and white '56 Chevy Bel Air, "Zebra", with a Corvette 327 and three on the tree. It was a trip to watch Don shift from first to second under racing pressure. He would literally THROW himself up into second and reel back into the seat. I thought the seat would break! Anyway, Don's Chevy was nice and fast. Gary Jinks had a green 1950 Olds Holiday 2-door Hardtop. Randy Rogers' dad, Si, bought it new in '50. It had a 303 OHV V/8 and a 3-speed manual transmission. Gary tweaked the Holiday, Rocket 88", with a 4 barrel carb and duals. He rebuilt the engine and increased the compression ratio, thereby increasing the horsepower. The "Rocket" ran well! One of our buds, Ed Nowaski, had a '54 Chevy 210 sedan. He tweaked the 235 six with twin carbs, a high lift cam, and a split exhaust manifold and duals. I think

Ed's car was named "Six Shooter"! It ran good, but not good enough to get by "Black Thunder's" 276 FLATHEAD!! HaHa! Of course, we both could give a new 265 Chevy a run for the money! Gordon Reddy had a cherry '57 Chevy BelAir 2door hardtop, Baby Baby". After Gordon beefed it up including a 4-speed Hydramatic from an Olds, it ran really well. John Braswell had a hard-running red and white '55 Chevy, "Lightnin", 2 door BelAir. Tommy Boyd's '61 Chevy Super Sport, "Mariah", was super clean and sported a blower that Tommy added. Wayne Miller (Jan Clements' boyfriend) had a metallic green '53 Ford Sunliner convertible, "Lil Darlin", with twin carbs, Edelbrock aluminum heads, and overdrive! We also had Barry Palmer's '34 Ford five-window blue coupe, "Dreamer", with a Merc mill and 2 deuces. Of course Dickie's '54 Chevy, Honey Bun", was always a favorite. We also had the Reid twins, Peggy and Tommy, with their green, '49 Chevy fastback, The Turtle". It wasn't fast, but it was steady and dependable. We also had Sheila's "Grey Goose", her granny's '52 Plymouth Belvedere 4-door sedan. Then we had Sonny's pink and white, beautiful '55, Fairlane, and Barb's Chariot". Another was Mark Lamkin's, Runnin' Bare", a tan '50 Ford Tudor. Not to be forgotten, we had Dan Rogers' '51, green, Ford Victoria, "Green Hornet", and Dwight Duncan's super sharp, green, '55 Chevy BelAir hardtop, "Tadpole". Also was Norman Roberts' '52 yellow Chevy BelAir convertible, with a yellow and black interior, "Tops Down". Included was Don Gordon's '58 Chevy Impala, "White Lightnin". We even had one classmate, Jimmy Johnson, who had a red '57 Ford Fairlane 500 hardtop named "Cathy's Clown". In short order he had Cathy replaced with Cindy, not only in the name but in the front seat as well! Think he had a thing for girls with "C" names! There were tons of other cars but these are the local ones with names I can remember!

So, all in all, we kids enjoyed a fabulous time when cars were unique when the horsepower race was "on" for the manufacturers when cars could be modified rather inexpensively and by us, and when lack of traffic, and partially completed divided highways made for plentiful "playgrounds" of concrete and asphalt.

Great times,
Danny

49

A Cool Car Story

Circa 1959. Mostly true!

Please indulge me as I must add this little tale told to me by two, very reputable sources, independent and apart from each other, at separate times, totally confirming the other's version. Although I didn't live the event with them, the story sure got my attention. These two guys, Ray Davis and Jerry Caddell, were good buds, Colts, and about five years my senior. I became friends with both men and it's such a good car story I had to share it with you. Some of the information was a little sketchy, so, ever so slightly, I may have had to improvise a little. Please forgive me, but the essence of the story is sacred.

As the story goes, one Saturday night our guys were looking for some new drag race victims, so they decided to visit Sivils Drive-in, in Dallas. Like PALs, Sivils was a hangout for the younger set, many of whom had fast cars. It was well known that a few bucks might be made engaging in some extracurricular street racing, picked up at Sivils. Of course, that is, if you selected an opponent that you could likely beat! They took Ray's red, 1957 Chevy 2-door sedan ("Lil' Red Wagon")

151

because Ray wanted to drive and he thought his car was faster than Jerry's '51 Victoria, and besides, Jerry drove last time! Ray's car was very much a "sleeper" as it had steel wheels and "dog dish" small hubcaps. He had removed all the typical V/8 emblems and had hidden dual exhausts with cut-outs. Under the hood, it had a fuel-injected Corvette engine paired with a close-ratio four-speed and a 4:11 positrac rear axle. Hidden within the rear wheel wells were a set of fresh Bucrons and traction bars. This "Wagon" could haul the mail! We're talking 14-second quarter times and a top end of about 125.

Shortly after their arrival to Sivils, a fellow in a turquoise '58 Chevy Impala equipped with a 348, 3 deuces and a Turboglide, engaged them to a $20.00 run. Our boys took the bet and proceeded to follow the Impala to a secluded part of the newly poured, 635 loop around Dallas, still unfinished and not yet open for public use. The locals knew a way to move a few barricades and access this part of the highway. This part of the highway had already been marked with a start line, a quarter-mile finish line and a one-mile finish line. The car lights were the only illumination so a few carloads of kids came to watch and helped light up the raceway. The drivers got ready and up to the start line. The local flag girl sent them off, tires squalling! Ray got the jump on the Impala and the Impala never caught Ray due in part to the lower axle ratio of the '57 as well as inefficiencies of the '58s Turboglide.

So everyone piled in their cars and returned to Sivils. Our boys were feeling pretty confident as the cars rolled back into the drive-in. Also, not to be minimized, they'd won $20.00! After a burger and a Coke, they noticed a pale yellow '57 T-Bird circling the drive-in. It had unusual, plain steel wheels, no hubcaps, and black wall tires. Something else that was unusual, it was summertime and the bird had the removable hardtop, with porthole windows still in place. Funny circumstances on a hot summer night.

The T-Bird pulled right up beside Ray's '57. The name on the side of the Bird was "Tweety Bird". The boys began jawing back and forth and ultimately agreed upon an unusual contest. The first leg of the race was to the 1/4 mile marker for $50.00. The second leg of the race was to the mile marker for $100.00. Our guys had never seen a T-Bird that could begin to hang with either of their cars. Even if this one was exceptional on the top end, Ray would be so far ahead at the 1/4 marker, going 90 or so, with 30 more MPH to go, the Bird couldn't possibly catch him in 30 seconds or so. By then the red Chevy would be over the mile marker, right? They took the wager! This would be a $170.00 night!

Once again a bunch of carloads followed them out to the raceway. This time there were more carloads. Our boys looked at each other and almost simultaneously said "Good gosh, this Bird guy must know a lot of people, you think he's done this before?"

Ok, same drill at the beginning of the race as Ray jumped the Bird by a length or so. Ray kept saying "We'll be pulling away real soon"! All the way through first, second, third, and just into fourth, the Bird was on Ray's back bumper. At that time our guys crossed the 1/4 mile marker. They won! One more leg. Of course, Ray's right food was slammed to the floor and the Chevy was pulling strong, headed quickly for 125 MPH. The Bird can't catch us, they both thought. The Chevy was running like a top that night. About that time, the Bird blew by them like a fighter jet, as if they were standing still. By the time they passed the mile marker the taillights on the Bird were tiny dots. Our guys lost $30.00, but worse, got embarrassed along the way. They did, however, learn a good lesson about factory-blown 312 T-Birds that night, for future reference! "Tweety Bird" had the 340 HP racing version with an overdrive transmission. One of the fastest street cars in Dallas at the time. Tweety could fly!

Thanks my friends,
Danny

Cars of the 1950s:
The American Love Affair
with the Automobile

To understand the changes that evolved in the '50s we have to understand the post-WWII mindset of the population. Essentially all U.S. auto production halted as our car factories were turned into war machinery factories making Jeeps, tanks, personnel carriers, aircraft engines and other necessary war items. USA production of new cars shut down in 1942. Hundreds of thousands of our young men were shipped off and into many different countries and battle zones. As young soldiers, far from home their key subjects of conversations turned to girls and cars. A lot of the guys were exposed to sports cars. Small, two-seaters, but nimble machines with floor shift transmissions and convertible tops. Some were powerful, some were not but all handled well and could corner with speed. What a change from what was available in the States at the time. The guys liked it and yearned for something similar.

So, when the war was over in 1945, the US car makers have faced with a significant challenge as well as a huge opportunity: "Design new and attractive cars for these returning heroes who had money to spend and a pent-up appetite for new and exciting cars". It took a little while, but the car makers got up to speed and produced some new models for 1947, however, most companies produced the pre-war 1942 models until 1949. The older pre-war models were stodgy designs, had very pronounced fenders of the '30s, were dull colors, and were, generally, underpowered and not exciting to drive. The new models had to be sleek, with exciting new colors and interiors, with V8 power, and more accessories and options.

Studebaker, the oldest American car company at that time, was the first with a new body design for 1947, but still had the same old engines. Cadillac was next with newly designed 1948 bodies with WWII aircraft simulated tail fins. Also new for 1947 and 1948 was a brand new car company, Tucker. It was a radical new design utilizing a converted helicopter engine in the rear and a "cyclops" center, swivel headlight. Sadly they only lasted two years. The next year Cadillac and Oldsmobile each brough new, lighter and more powerful V8 engines for the 1949 model year. Olds got a new body and a new model name, Rocket 88. Chevy, Pontiac and Buick got new body designs as well in 1949. Ford, Mercury and Lincoln got new body designs including convertible hardtops, as well as more powerful engine designs soon thereafter. The Chrysler Corporation cars, Plymouth, Dodge, DeSoto and Chrysler were a little slow as far as new body designs were concerned, however, Chrysler came to market with a new, highly efficient and powerful engine design called the "Hemi" in 1951. All Chrysler products had modern engines as well as newly designed, modern body designs by 1955. Imperials even had "bomber sight" taillights. Chevy and Pontiac finally got modern V8 power as well as redesigned bodies in 1955. Packard and Rambler were modernized as well. The race for power and speed was a large factor, as evidenced across the board.

A milestone car was unveiled by Chevy in 1953. It was the Corvette. The first true American sports car. It was a two-seater with a much more powerful engine than the typical Chevy. It was a great start, available in one color, white. By 1957 the Corvette was a powerhouse with fuel injection and a four-speed. Ford also came to market in 1955 with a more personal two-seat roadster called the Thunderbird. It was more of a "Gentleman's Sports Car" than the Corvette, however, by 1957, it was available with more power than the Corvette. By 1958 it became a luxury personal car.

Chrysler battled GM through the '50s for the "King of Tailfins" title. Cadillac finally won In 1959 with the massive tailfins and twin bullet taillights on their models. All car makers were modernized by about 1957.

So goes the story of the cars of the '50s. A glorious time in automotive history! Beautiful bodies, record-setting sales, innovative engineering, awesome color combinations, multiple carburetors, superchargers, fuel injection, luxurious interiors (even some with bucket seats), huge power and floor shift 4-speed trannys! What could be better?? Nothing!!

IMHO,
Danny

51

Summer Job @ LTV, 1963

It was the summer of 1963, I had just graduated AHS and was anticipating a fun-filled summer. The admissions process had proven successful, so I was looking forward to being a resident of Texas A&M for the second time in my young life.

My little family had lived there in university housing right across the street from Kyle Field, in 1946 and in 1947, after my dad returned home from an Army Infantry tour of France and Germany in WWII. He went in as a Second Lieutenant and came out a Captain with a Purple Heart. He once told me he became a Captain because all his superiors had gotten killed. He was reluctant to ever talk about the war like so many Vets.

I wanted to enjoy the summer, buy a better car, and put a few bucks back for college away from home. In order to do so a few dollars would need to be generated by a good job. I was lucky enough to secure one at LTV, thanks to Mrs. Boyd, Tommy's mom, and at that time, the "gatekeeper" for many jobs and new employees. She was a super nice lady and helped many an AHS student looking for a good job. My dad worked there, too, and knew Mrs. Boyd, which certainly didn't hurt either.

The job I got was being a "lamper" on the second shift. The second shift started at 4:45 PM and we got off at 12:30 AM. A "lamper's" duties included the changing or replacement of failed lighting. Since most of the office workers had left before our shift began, we could more efficiently do our job without interfering with theirs. Since the company was unionized, it was not acceptable for an office worker to change their own light bulb, therefore, every light fixture in the entire facility had to be repaired or entirely replaced by us via a maintenance work request. Just imagine a place big enough to house a total of 12,000 folks including executives and their staff, engineering and their staff, administrators and their staff, machinists to make the parts for jet fighters, and the space required for assemblers and technicians to assemble them. In only one location we're talking about 20 very large buildings, 20 smaller buildings, in excess of two million square feet under the roof, and 20 acres of employee parking. (Please understand that these are very gross estimates). Anyway, the point is that LTV was huge at that time and that It took a full-time team to keep up with burned-out light bulbs!

Our three-man team was comprised of an electrician named Jeremy Watt, an electrician apprentice named Voltameer Ready, we called him "Volt", and yours truly, who named me "Lightnin", as I was the quick newbie in the group. We were part of a fairly large group of maintenance electricians under the leadership of Ellis Sodd. We were assigned a little yard tractor-type vehicle that could carry many supplies and was powerful enough to pull a trailer when needed as we went all over the facility. We went into some of the most luxurious executive offices imaginable, even some with private bathrooms. I was impressed! We serviced lots of offices and even the cafeteria. We took care of the machine shop and the quality control center, as well.

But one night we got a service order to replace four lights in the "high bay" area of the fighter assembly line. We had driven through that area a hundred times and marveled at the height required for the aircraft. That ceiling must have been 80-100 feet tall. Amazing! Even more amazing was that there were huge lights mounted to the ceiling structure. BUT NOW, we were looking at bulb replacement in some of those lights! That will get your attention.

In the electrical supply yard, there was a little trailer that had, essentially, a hook and ladder-type telescoping ladder attached to it. The trailer also had extendable stabilizer arms and pads that could help support the apparatus when the tele-scoping ladder was extended. (I'm sure you've got the picture). When we hooked up to the trailer I noticed that along the side of the trailer, someone had cleverly stenciled the name "Widowmaker"! Nice! Now, it just so happened that just be-fore coming to work ol' Watt had eaten some shrimp that were beginning to talk back to him, so he was a little queasy. If that wasn't bad enough, Volt had somewhat sprained his ankle play-ing flag football the day before. Uh oh, Lightnin's turn at bat. I was scared but I wouldn't show it! We got "Widowmaker" in place to address the first light and extended the stabilizers. There was a little platform at the top of the ladder with a safety handrail around it. There was barely room for me and the huge bulb. I got on, we loaded the light and they began to extend the telescoping ladder. Holy cow, it kept going up! I kept ask-ing myself "What would Hirsch do"? I didn't yell but sure wanted to. We finally reached the top the whole thing began to sway, almost lifting up the back wheels! The guys down below hopped on the back of the trailer and the swaying subsided. I moved very slowly from that point on. I managed to get the burned-out bulb removed and put the new one in place. Done! I couldn't get down quick enough. What a day, I mean night!

It was a good night of team building and I began to understand that you are nothing without the friends around you! It was a good summer and I got that next car!!

Thanks, team,
Danny

52

The Sweetest 1955 Chevy! Blue Velvet!

Summer 1963. Arlington, Texas

In the summer of 1963, it was time to move up the food chain to a hotter ride. The 1949 Ford "Black Thunder" had served her purpose well; 44W/15L, with zero losses to opponents in the same general category. Sadly, we lost to a few cars out of our class. At any rate, time to raise the bar. Here comes "Blue Velvet"! She was a light blue 1955 Chevy BelAir two-door sedan. I bought her from Jimmy Hovers for $650.00. Jimmy's dad owned Jay's Radiator shop on the East Division. She had a later model Corvette engine with a 2.20 low, close-ratio four-speed tranny and a 3.36 posi rear end. It was a great set-up for a highway car. She had an AFB carb and a 30/30 'Vette cam. Although a small engine she had lots of heart, and she was an exceptional runner. Many a car with a bigger engine had to bow in her presence!

The Little 283 engine would wind to 8000 RPM but on most occasions, I'd shift at 7200 RPM. The beauty of that combination, was that at a 35 MPH rolling start, preferred by 327 Chevy Powerglide or 383 Plymouth/Dodge automatics of the day, I could hammer them all the way to 70 MPH in low gear, then leave them behind in the second. "Velvet" could go 85 in second and 110 In third! Fourth was good for another 15 MPH or so. Lots of fun!! Many nights I left PAL's, floored "Velvet" north on Fielder to West Second up to 80 or so, braked hard and turned left, turned off the ignition, and ditched the lights. Then I slithered her into our drive and glided on the grass to the rear of the garage. The cops didn't have a unit that could catch me or find me!

I took her to A&M with me in the fall of 1963. She brought me home safely many weekends. I've never had as many relatives die that semester at A&M! I think one Grandmother died three times! There was one weekend in particular that I remember well. It was Friday, November 22nd and I was in Sbisa Dining hall at A&M. The freshmen were eating "square" meals in tiny bites. Tiny bites were necessary as we had to be ready to answer upperclassmen's questions. At any rate, we were preparing for the upcoming bonfire activities which included cutting mass quantities of lumber, all scheduled to begin the next morning. We were almost finished with lunch when the loudspeaker came on and it was announced that our President had been shot in Dallas. Silence, then pandemonium. Several hours later, the powers in charge canceled all the weekend activities and sent all of us home for the weekend. There were three guys that wanted a ride back to the Fort Worth area. We all piled into "Velvet" and headed north. It was already dark when we left College Station. We were flying low to say the least. The Chevy speedometer only went to 110 and read a little fast, so we were bumping up against the peg literally all the way home. There was one stretch of old Highway 6, north of Marlin, headed toward Reisel where the little two-lane country highway crossed three tributaries to the Brazos. Anyway, we were coming up on the little bridges that crossed those creeks. They each had a little rise or bump if you will.

I had crossed them many times previously at about 80. The steering got light but "Velvet" settled in smoothly. Tonight we were rocking about 90 and I wondered how she'd do. We went over bridge one. Not too bad, just a little squirrely. All of a sudden I hear a sniveling from the back seat. I looked back. There was Jerry, in the floorboard of the back seat curled up like a dog, whimpering! I considered letting off a little, but hey, a new world record was at stake! I floored it! The speedo was now hammered against the 110 peg for a couple of minutes! The second bridge felt like a roller coaster cresting the pinnacle! Now the third! Awesome! We were rolling toward a new record! Well, needless to say, Jerry never asked me for another ride home!!

Anyway, "Velvet" served me well although Becky could never get her into or out of reverse!!

Thanks for the memories, Velvet!
Danny

Marilyn:
The One That Got Away!

Circa 1964

It was the fall of 1964. I had a good job as a machinist at LTV. I think I was making $2.75 per hour, but had great benefits! That was a good job back then. I was making parts for fighter aircraft. I had a nice 1955 Chevy BelAir with a later-model Corvette engine. It was a lot of fun!

My good friend, Gary Jinks, was part of a "car family", including his Dad Joe Jinks, who was a wheeler-dealer and a true character, as well his Mom, Iva Lois, a sweetheart, his older sis Anita, who drove a turquoise '56 T-Bird, and Joe Dale, Gary's older brother, by about five years, who really knew cars and especially high-performance models. Thank goodness for Anita, as far as Iva Lois was concerned, helping her retain her sanity with those three guys! Mr. Jinks and Joe Dale always called me by my last name, but not so with Anita, Gary, and Mrs. Jinks. I was over there a lot drooling over Joe Dell's latest acquisition. At any rate, they lived on Bluebonnet Trail, just a little west of South Davis Elementary School. They were in a great neighborhood with the Carlsons across the street, Billy Crane's family next door, and the Pucellas around the corner, as well as the Hirsches, Overalls, Rhineharts, Coders, with Rosalyn Rosemond further down the street on Tulip Drive. A very cool neighborhood, to say the least.

Back to the story. In October of '64, Joe Dale had purchased a '57 Corvette at an auction in Dallas. It happened to be a fuel-injected, 283 HP, 4 speed, positraction, and was red and white, an absolute dream! I wanted it! I needed it! I could visualize driving her in a myriad of situations. Fun, fun, fun! Conveniently, I was not yet married so a wife's approval was not needed. I was ready to cut a deal with Joe Dale to buy it, but, before I could get it it done, "Marilyn" had an engine fire. (I named her Marilyn because she was beautiful, fast and ready for excitement). The fire had melted some of her engine components and ruined her hood, among other things. Nothing that an enterprising young man couldn't handle, I thought.

Somehow, the 'Vette was totaled by the insurance company and sold for salvage. It's beyond me how, but a local, somewhat questionable dealer of used car parts, Jerry F., ended up with my "Marilyn"! Now, Gary had some dealings with Jerry and he was apparently friends with Joe Dale, as well. I knew Jerry but had never had any direct dealings with him. Other local car guys had experienced some, not so satisfying dealings, with Jerry, but I had to chance it! At any rate, I contacted Jerry and made a deal to purchase the defiled, somewhat battered, abused, and in-distress "Princess". Our agreed-upon price was $200.00 cash. I gathered up the cash, borrowed a car trailer, with all the tools and equipment needed to get her on the trailer and then headed toward Oak Cliff, Jerry's new hunting grounds, with my bud Gary.

We got to Jerry's house, rang the bell and Jerry came out. After cordial greetings, Jerry proceeded to inform us that he had reconsidered, and had decided not to sell "Marilyn". A little extra cash didn't sway him from the decision. She was out of reach, and it was beyond my control! I was heartbroken, however; old enough to realize that things don't always work out the way you want them to, and usually for the best end result. This was one of those times but no easier to swallow. It was a long drive home.

Oh Marilyn, all the fun times we could have enjoyed together! It was wishful thinking for another day! But you never know, someday we may meet again. I can only hope!

Thanks "Marilyn" for the dreams,
Danny

54

AHS, Class of 1963

Every class is different and unique. It's natural that each class believes that they are special; however, I contend that we actually have a basis for claiming a unique station in the evolution of the American Way as it pertains to the alumni of AHS. Sure, there were great classes before and after our class, but are they comparable? Perhaps, but not a prayer in these eyes!

My contention is that we were the perfect blend of old and new, of country and rock and roll, of hip and old school, of Boy Scouts and thugs, of jocks and gear heads, of Honor Society members and slackers, of prom queens and pink ladies, of Future Farmers and musicians. What an interesting mix! We were so lucky! Classes before and after seemed to have less diversity, which yielded less overall conflict and interest. Of course, that is purely a biased opinion!

I think that the birth years of 1944, '45 & '46 yielded pent-up, superior genetics that resulted in our success and dominance. Likely the result of the genetic phenomenon appropriately named the "Anti-Hitler Genome". Of course, there have been major scientific studies confirming this phenomenon, but I won't bore you with that proven information.

In that regard, we can't help that we are "The King of the Hill" as far as scientifically speaking, in the history of AHS, IMHO! Now, I own some oceanfront properties In Arizona if you are buying all that!

Thank you very much!!
Danny

Upperclassmen

*Our 1961 and 1962 AHS upperclass Colt
Brothers and Sisters! What great role models!*

Don't think I've ever taken the opportunity to express my gratitude for you Colts of the classes of '61 & '62, but let me try. Thank you! Looking back, many of you were literally big brothers and sisters to many of us younger AHS "siblings". I guess it's commonplace for younger classmen and classwomen to look up to their seniors; however, having such a great bunch of kids to follow behind was a little overwhelming!! So, thank you very much for setting the bar so high. At that time, Arlington was growing leaps and bounds, and so was the Colt tradition and community. You guys literally set the stage with Act 1 of the '60s and you led us to Act 2.

In looking back to those times and remembering the folks that meant most to me, I'm reminded that the line gets a little fuzzy between the folks that you admired, envied, was attracted to, were jealous of, were a better version of you, were more athletic, were a better musician or actor, or perhaps were more popular. And hey, we had a bunch to choose from!! AHS had them all!!

You each have your own folks that you looked up to but for me they are as follows in no particular order: Mike Farhat, always a friendly face and a firm handshake; Roger and Richard Huebner, great neighbors and friends; Steve Jackson, a ball player supreme; Sonny Wooten, a strong shoulder to lean on, anytime; Bruce Malone, Mr. Everything; Beverly Caddell, just an absolute dream; Robert Young, a very cool dude; Dickie Carmichael, another cool dude; Harry Allison, a great guy and down to earth; Charlie Clawson, a solid friend; Dennis Niles, always there; Kay King, a true dream girl; Curtis Buchanan, an old, old friend; Anita Jinks, the girl with the T-Bird; Kenny Watkins, a real amigo; Harold Prather, solid; Bonnie BeeBee, a sweetheart; Steve East, a friend forever; Johnny Watson, an old Cub Scout buddy; Linda Scanlon, yeah, admiration; Johnny Wright, a car dude. There are many others. Best wishes and many thanks to you all!!

Your admiring friend,
Danny

56

Music of the '50s & '60s

*In Arlington, we were blessed with the greatest music
(and radio DJs like Ron Chapman on KLIF) growing up
in the '50s & '60s, but I especially enjoyed those
"Car Songs" of the day!!*

Now, just to be clear, we had so many wonderful pop, rock and roll, crooners and country/western performers we could enjoy, and they were far too numerous for this guy to cover in a short story. However, my favorite "Car Songs", to sing along with, windows open and the radio blaring, narrow the field significantly, so here goes.

OK, let's get it started with "Rocket 88", a cool song in the early '50s, by Ike Turner and Jackie Brenston about the Oldsmobile model starting in 1949, touting the performance virtues of a small body and a big engine (the first muscle car, and the first Rock & Roll recording). The key line was "My real gone Rocket"! Also, "boozin' and cruzin' along", It was number one on the charts! What a song to sing along with and to get this story started!!

Next on the lineup is "Hot Rod Lincoln", one of my personal favorites and a pre-selected, funeral song! Originally recorded by Charley Ryan in 1955, it told the story of a young hot-rodder that had surgically implanted a large Lincoln engine into a lightweight Model A Ford coupe. Lots of wonderful lyrics but my favorite is "Son, you're gonna drive me to drinkin' if you don't stop drivin' that Hot Rod Lincoln!" Loved it!

Third up is "The Ballad of Thunder Road", a song sung by Robert Mitchum and tied to the 1958 film by the same name, starring, who else but Robert Mitchum! He played the part of a Tennessee bootlegger with a special, souped up transport car, trying to outrun the revenuers. Exciting car chases for that time period! My personal favorite lyrics were: "There was thunder, thunder, over Thunder Road, Thunder was his engine and white light'nin was his load". Also: "The law they never got him 'cause the devil got him first"! All sing!

Fourth is The Beach Boys hit from '62, "409"! What a song to sing along with! (Wanted a '61 SS 409 so bad, but, so far, never got it.) Of course the song referred to a '62 with dual quads, as they weren't available in '61. Naturally, she had a 4-speed and positraction. Many a fun evening was had singing along to that with my buds!

Fifth is the 1955, Chuck Berry song, "Maybellene". What a memorable song, a 130 hp Ford trying to chase down a 230 hp Coupe de Ville on the open road. The Caddy was rollin' 'bout 110. Darn that girl, she could drive but she just couldn't be true! Let's face it, Chuck was either dreaming or smoking something for him to imagine that his Ford could catch that Caddy! Great song though!

Sixth on the car hit parade is the 1963 Beach Boys song, "Little Deuce Coupe". One of their best and most listened to. Mind you this was a 4-speed, hopped up, "Flathead" powered '32 Ford that could do 140 MPH! Now that's pretty amazing. And, "she could walk a Thunderbird like it was standing still"! Loved singing along with that one!

Seventh is the 1964 rendition of "Little GTO", by Ronny and the Daytonas. Now Ronny's little 3 deuce, 4-speed GTO was not only excellent on the drag strip but also dominated the road course circuits. Wow, his must have been the only '64 GTO in existence to do that!! Best sing along lyrics were "turn it on, wind it up, blow it out, GTO!!"

Eight is Jan and Dean's, '64 song, "The Little Old Lady from Pasadena". She kept that brand new, shiny red, Super Stock Dodge ready for action on Colorado Boulevard! With a four-speed and a 4:56 out back, coupled to a 426 under the hood, she was hard to beat stoplight to stoplight!! "Go Granny, go Granny, go Granny, go!!"

Number nine is "Fun, Fun, Fun", a 1963 song by The Beach Boys. The girl driver was having fun, fun, speeding around town in her dad's car, not going to the library as intended. The lyrics go, "She'll have fun, fun, fun until her Daddy takes the T-bird away". Then later in the song dad obviously took away the car and the lyrics change to, "We'll have fun, fun, fun, since her Daddy took the T-bird away"! Great to sing along with!

A few others are:

"Dead Man's Curve" by Jan and Dean

"Mustang Sally" by Wilson Pickett

"Shut Down" by The Beach Boys

Those are my favorites. Bet you have some too!

Danny

57

A Local Gathering Spot

The Cooper Street Car Wash. Arlington, Texas 1963.

My good friend, Bill Woodman, designed, built and opened the Cooper Street Car Wash in 1963. It was one of the first coin-operated, self-service, car washes in Arlington. It was located at the corner of South Cooper and Grant Street, just a block north of Park Row. It had four wash bays and a vacuum station at the rear. A quarter would buy the customer five minutes of wash/rinse time and a dime would operate the vacuum for five minutes, as well. Bill was a car enthusiast and an engineer so he was careful about selecting the right equipment and soaps to perform the best job for his cars as well as the customers' vehicles. Because of Bill's attention to detail, outgoing personality and true interest in the customers and their cars, the car wash became an oasis for car enthusiasts and was very successful.

Most folks called him simply Woodman, but I called him Bill since I'd known him several years before he opened the car wash as he was in our church, First Presbyterian, and being an Aggie he was friends with my Dad. Bill had a knack of relating to people significantly older as well as younger. Maybe it was the car connection but I've never known anyone with that broad and age span of friends. He was unique in many ways as he loved antique as well as modern music players and instruments as well as beautiful landscaping. His appreciation of fine craftsmanship overflowed way beyond automotive restoration quality into architecture, hand-crafted furniture, photography and many other interests. His sense of humor was delightful and his bold laugh was contagious. He was a great friend to many and I was one of those lucky folks.

Aside from PAL's, the A&P parking lot across the street, the other PAL's and the Bull Pen, the car wash was a natural gathering place for car guys. The array of vehicles was astounding! From whatever special car Joe Dale Jinks had at the time, to Don Smith's 'Vette, to John Donaghy's perfect '63 1/2, white Galaxy 500 XL. To Blesi's Mustang, Dickie's Corvair, Wayne Miller's green '53 Ford Sunliner, Mobley's 750 Honda 4, Gary's green "Rocket 88", Dwight's '55 Chevy, Hickson's Black '57 convertible, Charles Richey's '56 Chevy, Stewart's Grand Prix, Nowaski's black Chevy, Tommy's black and blown '61 bubble top, Jacque's '57 T-Bird, Steve East's '53 Ford, Duppy's Stude, Braswell's '55 Chevy, Sonny's '55 Ford, Randy's Pontiac, Sutherland's Falcon, Gordon's beautiful Desert Rose, '57 BelAir, Wayne's Lark, Andy's Chevy II, Tommy's '59 Chevy, Becky's black and white '56 Chevy, and multitudes of others. Many cars were bought and sold from the car wash parking lot, as well were many after-market, hot rod parts. I heard tell that even a few competition experiments were arranged!

There are two days I'll never forget. First is when Charles Eller, with a couple of his running buds, Johnson and LeQuay, showed up in Charles' brand new, Wimbledon White, R code, 4-speed 1964 Galaxy 500 XL, a beautiful beast of a car! Next was when the Rash brothers, Doug and Dwight, rolled up in a '62 red Pontiac Catalina, equipped with a Super Duty 421 with dual quads, 4-speed, aluminum body parts, a Swiss cheese frame, and aluminum headers with a factory cut-out exhaust. It was a street-legal race car! Now those were BIG days!

All in all, a lot of great times with great friends were had at Woodman's Cooper Street Car Wash!!

Thanks, Bill! R.I.P., my friend!
Danny

It Was You & You & You!

BY DANNY ARMSTRONG

Arlington, Texas — after World War II,
What a special place for me and for you.
A quiet, little town — amid a growing metro center,
A town with one high school — with the heart of a winner.

You were there in Mrs. Houston's class,
And you were there when our bikes were fast.
You were there in Sunday school,
and yes, you were there when ducktails were cool.

You were there for a Chuck Wagon meal,
After Little League games, "Did you pick off a steal?"
You were there at Scout Club Meetings,
And you were there for Training Union greetings.

It was you at The Jet, roller skates smokin',
And it was you at the Fair, winning those tokens.
It was you in history and you in math,
And it was you and me that reaped the teacher's wrath.

It was you at the play and you in the band.
It was you at the game and who held my hand.
'Twas you at Lucas and you at the show,
And it was you who yearned to be in the know.

All of the memories stick like glue.
The number one reason is You & You & You!
It was you at the lake on water skis,
And it was you at the park, kite in the breeze.

It was you in the huddle, on the football team,
Trying like us all, to fulfill a dream.
Yes, it was you, looking so pretty at the high school dance,
And it was me wishing for just half a chance.

It was you in the race behind the wheel,
Driving like crazy as tires let out a squeal.
And it was you, there at Feather Beach,
With a warm summer tan and hair so bleached.

Yes, you are why I love to recall,
Yes, you are the best reason of all!!
And you are the reason I love to remember.
Just hope I can recall, come next December!

Best Memories,
Danny

Remember The Past, Enjoy the Moment

BY DANNY ARMSTRONG

Arlington High School of our past,
How could we know, those times wouldn't last?
We were so busy trying to be older,
We took chances to prove we were bolder.

Our parents were stuffy and OH so glaring,
It took us time to know they were caring.
We were so young, dreams of a party;
None could consider life after forty.

Some went to War, some had kids,
Some went to school and some hit the skids.
Some moved away, others stayed in town,
Some became teachers, others stayed clowns.

Some became lawyers, doctors, and clerks,
Others grew up to be salesmen and jerks.

Girls, boys, sports and cars,
fads, fashion, songs and wars,

Those were topics long ago,
Before maturity said, "Hello".

Now we've advanced somewhat in years,
But I'm not so sure 'bout 'tween the ears.
We seem old and set in our ways,
To our kids on the wave of the latest rage.

"Take care not to speed and buckle up"
These are the chants we give as our kids grow up.
What would you change if you could go back?
Would you take typing again or run with the pack?

Would you try out for the ball or play in the band?
Would you take out Miss Right and hold her hand?
Would you work for an "A" or try for a "B",?
Would you go for a record or settle for a "C"
Would you spit out your thoughts or hold them in?
Would you do again what you did back then?

As for me and I bet for most of you,
Little would change to go back in view.

How could we know those days wouldn't last?
How could we know each yesterday was "THE PAST"?
Those days should be treasured one by one,
Each friend remembered as we had fun.

So enjoy the night and the rest of your time,
And remember these subjects etched in our minds.

Girls, boys, sports and cars,
Fads, fashion, songs, and wars.

Those were the topics long ago,
And probably will be — for as long as we know.

Remember and enjoy!
Danny

Wishing

BY DANNY ARMSTRONG

Arlington Texas ---------circa 1963,
Oh, what an incredible place to be.
Looking back it's such a blur,
We didn't know then how lucky we were.

We had no worries about drugs or crime,
We had teachers that cared and could give the time.
You could get around town on a bike or a scooter
Not having to care about traffic and commuters.

There were a handful of grade schools, with local games
All neatly arranged- most with "Directional" names.
Two junior highs were all we knew
Ousley's red and white and Carter's white and blue.

Only one high school in our neat little town
Meant we would all be together on common ground.
Arlington back then was about 30,000 strong But the
Friday night game was the place to belong.

PAL'S was the local burger drive-in
Where everyone went to meet up with friends.
Cars were hot back in '63
So were the races on Spur 303.

We all had big dreams way back then,
But the paths of life take some interesting bends.
Some became Doctors, lawyers, and engineers
Some became teachers, builders, and volunteers.

Some got married some went to war.
Some went to college some to the bar
Isn't it funny how we all changed
Yet in so many ways were still the same.
If I had only one wish — it would be....

Back in Arlington — Circa 1963

61

It Is "The Story of Our Lives," the AHS Class of 1963

We were, indeed, at the right place at the right time. Arlington was a dynamic college town, with amazing civic and educational leaders. Our one and only high school was blessed with post-war, absolutely awesome administrators, teachers, coaches, and families, including us kids! What a place to be a part of and to cherish. We also had exceptional civic leaders and churches. All in all, we had it ALL! Our time was unlike any before, and likely any since. IMHO, the stars lined up for us, my friends! Thank you all for being a part of my experiences.

That first bike ride; that first "special" smile; that first Cub Scout meeting; that first base hit; that first horse ride; that first call to the principal's office; that first picnic date; that first job selling donuts; that first go-cart; that first 400 relay; that first country club dance; that first (and only) important tackle; that first car club project; that first crush; that first theme paper that exceeded a "C"; that first kiss; that first (and only) no-hitter; that first shrimp cocktail; that first touchdown; that first shop project; that first stick-shift driving lesson; that first car date; that first AHS pep rally; and that first realization that this was as good as it gets!

Thank you all!
Danny

Song Titles Tale

The songs of the '50s and '60s told from the perspective of an Arlington, Texas homeboy. It's meant only for your entertainment and reflections of memories!!

This is a completely fictitious tale about a kid from the 1960s telling the story of a long weekend. The story is intended to mask as many different song titles from the day as possible. There are 66 embedded in the story. How many can you find?? (Note: some of the titles are slightly modified or abbreviated).

After a leisurely late lunch at Fernando's Hideaway, Peggy Sue and I spent the afternoon sitting on the dock of the bay, then we hopped in my hot rod Lincoln, with no particular place to go, and drove out to Kokomo Bay. When we got there, I couldn't unfasten her safety belt, but when I finally did, we walked on the beach and as the sun went down, we watched a beautiful sailboat with billowing red sails in the sunset. Later, under a blue moon, on the beach, I told her I wanted to hold her hand and she said yes! Before calling it a night, we serendipitously danced under the light of the silvery moon and wrote love letters in the sand. I stopped for a moment to pick up a sea shell and looking ahead, I saw poetry in motion as Peggy Sue walked ahead of me. It left me breathless! As we were walking back to the car in the starlight, we made plans to go on a sea cruise together in the summertime next year, upon my return. After I took her home, I pondered what our chances are and what might be our future. I got misty as I thought about it. We had to say goodbye as Peggy Sue was leaving for vacation tomorrow on a jet plane, with her family.

After dropping her off I went down to The Starlight Lounge and enjoyed a Margarita (made with the proper ingredient, tequila), with my old friend Leroy Brown, his uncle Big John and his friend Mike, he called The Muleskinner. Prior to going back home, we made plans for tomorrow. As I hit the rack that night, I thought, no doubt, it's a wonderful world! I was grateful for the magic moment Peggy Sue and I shared and looked forward to seeing her again. In the meantime, I knew all I have to do is dream to be with my teen angel and I began to think love is a many-splendored thing as we enjoyed our last dance of the evening, in the sand.

It's not for me to say, or rave on, but tomorrow's plans were yielding a certain smile! Jimmy (we called him Teddy Bear), had a little Deuce coupe, Jack had an SS 409 and I had my GTO (my other car). We were going to meet up at the A&P parking lot and then pick up Donna (our surfer girl), Maybelline, and Susie Q (she was a sweet little 16 this year). From there we were headed to the Hotel California where there was a concert with Johnny B. Goode and Cathy's Clown. Of course, we had to negotiate Dead Man's curve just before Surf City, but that was no problem as we'd done it before. Crazy, I thought, but, oh boy, that'll be the day to remember!

And it really was! I met a little old lady from Pasadena, there with her granddaughter, Barbara Ann, a seeming sweetheart but really the devil in disguise as I later found out, but it doesn't matter anymore. She was indeed unforgettable, but not in a good way! However, that's another story.

We stopped off at a place named LaBamba on the way home for refreshments and I did the twist, the stroll, and the hully gully, with strangers in the night. The last dance we got on down to the real nitty gritty! On our way out we noticed there was a beautiful outdoor fireplace out on the balcony, and while passing by, smoke got in our eyes.

I was already missing Peggy Sue on the way home, and I kept praying, let it be me. I kept repeating that I'll be seeing you. I indeed had the lovesick blues! End of story!!

Enjoy,
Danny

Para A

   1. Fernando's Hideaway

   2. Peggy Sue

   3. Sittin' on the dock of the bay

   4. Hot Rod Lincoln

   5. Kokomo

   6. Unfasten safety belt

   7. Red Sails in the Sunset

   8. Blue Moon

   9. Let me hold your hand

   10. In the Light of the Silvery Moon

   11. Love Letters in the Sand

   12. Poetry in Motion

   13. Breathless

   14. Sea Cruise

   15. Summertime

   16. Chances Are

   17. Misty

18. Leaving on a Jet Plane

Para B
1. Starlight Lounge
2. Tequila
3. Leroy Brown
4. Big John
5. Muleskinner
6. It's a Wonderful World
7. Magic Moment
8. All have to do is Dream
9. Teen Angel
10. Love is a Many Splendored Thing
11. Last Dance

Para C
1. Not for Me to Say
2. Rave On
3. Certain Smile
4. Teddy Bear
5. Little Deuce Coupe
6. 409
7. GTO
8. Donna
9. Little Surfer Girl
10. Maybelline
11. Susie Q
12. Sweet Little 16
13. Hotel California
14. Johnny B. Good
15. Cathy's Clown
16. Dead Man's Curve
17. Surf City

18. Crazy
19. Oh Boy
20. That'll be the Day

Para D

1. Little Old Lady
2. Barbar'Ann
3. Devil in Disguise
4. Doesn't Matter
5. Unforgettable

Para E

1. LaBamba
2. Twist
3. Stroll
4. Hully Gully
5. Stranger in the Night
6. Last Dance
7. Nitty Gritty
8. Smoke in your Eyes

Para F

1. Let it be
2. Let it be Me
3. I'll be Seeing You
4. Lovesick Blues

1951
1960
1962
1963

1st Grade

2nd Grade

3rd Grade